DEATH AND BEYOND

EDWIN L. WOOLSEY

authorHOUSE®

AuthorHouse™
1663 Liberty Drive
Bloomington, IN 47403
www.authorhouse.com
Phone: 833-262-8899

Published by AuthorHouse 06/22/2021

ISBN: 978-1-6655-2993-8 (sc)
ISBN: 978-1-6655-2994-5 (e)

Print information available on the last page.

All scriptures were taken from the King James Version of the Bible

DEDICATION

This book is dedicated to my son Seth who urged me to write because he believed that people needed to know.

Thank you, Buddy. I love you!

CONTENTS

Preface ix

Chapter 1   It's about Time... 1
Chapter 2   Judgment 11
Chapter 3   Paradise 25
Chapter 4   Resurrection from Death Sleep 39
Chapter 5   The Consummation 51
Chapter 6   But until Then... Mediation for the Dead 65
Chapter 7   Here We Go Again... A Hint of
                 Reincarnation 81

About the Author.. 93

PREFACE

"Search the scriptures; for in them ye think ye have eternal life: and they are they which testify of me (John 5:39)."

I am mystified by the disconnect between the amount of material in the Bible dealing with death and how very little Western theology relies on that body of Scripture to explain what happens when life ends. In a vague way, we assume to understand what occurs after our last breath, but do we really? Can we say with surety what happens next? Where precisely do we go, and when do we get there? Are we able to point to ancient authoritative sources and say, "See, here it is?" Due to the fuzzy nature or our ideas, I'm afraid our current religious concepts of the afterlife are an outgrowth of popular culture, religious songs, and anecdotal stories instead of solid biblical texts or early Judeo-Christian orthodoxy.

Personally, I think this quandary is a modern anomaly since medieval society was more familiar with the certainty of dying than we are. This disassociation with spiritual reality might be a product of advancements in science and medicine that give us a false notion of immortality; however, nothing could be farther from the truth. Unquestionably, we will all die, and guaranteed that fact, a knowledge of what immediately follows the cessation of life might be an asset worth having, not only for peace of mind here but also for advanced preparation until we get there, especially in faith-based groups like Christianity. If anyone should master the questions and answers dealing with the transition between life and death, it should be the Church.

Maybe the somber nature of death makes us avoid the subject, or possibly the opposite is true. Our ignorance of God's Word might be the reason death seems so cryptic and foreboding, thus creating our shortsighted denial. Regardless, Jesus admonished us to pull our heads from the sand, search the Scripture, and make sure that our doctrines actually match God's source material... hence the purpose of this book.

Despite learning many new details, you might not agree with everything written here, but prepare for the challenge of uncovering the truth yourself before the day comes when you need to know the ageless answers about "Death and Beyond!"

CHAPTER ONE

IT'S ABOUT TIME

Very little is established in religious circles regarding the exact sequence of events after death. Two verses that immediately come to mind are "And as it is appointed unto men once to die, <u>but after this the judgment</u> (Hebrews 9:27)," and "We are confident, I say, and willing rather to be absent from the body, and <u>to be present with the Lord</u>. 9Wherefore we labour, that, whether present or absent, we may be accepted of him. <u>10For we must all appear before the judgment seat of Christ; that every one may receive the things done in his body, according to that he hath done, whether it be good or bad</u> (2 Corinthians 5:8-10)."

While 2 Corinthians 5:8 does not name the location where we will be "present with the Lord," yet that unanswered question will be discussed later. However, without identifying the exact placement of our post-death residence, we should note that Hebrews 9:27 and 2 Corinthians 5:10 both mention judgment after death, with one exception for two individuals who bypass death without an opportunity for a subsequent life-review, "And the beast was taken, and with him the false prophet that wrought miracles before him, with which he deceived them

Edwin L. Woolsey

that had received the mark of the beast, and them that worshipped his image. <u>These both were cast alive into a lake of fire burning with brimstone</u> (Revelation 19:20)." Bypassing death and judgment, these two evil individuals will be consigned to eternal torment while they are still alive, but not so with their followers.

In the Last Days, people who follow the Antichrist will still experience a natural death and face an ultimate judgment, but without the possibility of being forgiven for their misplaced allegiance, "And the third angel followed them, saying with a loud voice, If any man worship the beast and his image, and receive his mark in his forehead, or in his hand, <u>10The same shall drink of the wine of the wrath of God, which is poured out without mixture into the cup of his indignation; and he shall be tormented with fire and brimstone in the presence of the holy angels, and in the presence of the Lamb: 11And the smoke of their torment ascendeth up for ever and ever: and they have no rest day nor night, who worship the beast and his image, and whosoever receiveth the mark of his name</u>' (Revelation 14:9-11)."

While "some men's sins are open beforehand, going before to judgment; and some men they follow after (1 Timothy 5:24)," yet all must be judged for deeds done in the mortal body whether their actions are apparent in this life or hidden until the next. However, the object of our investigation is the amount of time that transpires between death and judgment. If judgment immediately follows death, then the disembodied soul can be instantly assigned to their eternal reward (which is presently impossible without the prerequisite of the resurrection which will be discussed later). Thus, an interval transpires between death, resurrection, and pending judgment, requiring the human spirit to be harbored someplace during the interim, but where? Obviously, Heaven cannot be granted or Perdition assigned, until after the resurrection, a subsequent life review, and God's verdict which comprise the judgment process.

Apart from the Antichrist and his False Prophet at the end of time, everyone else will face evaluation after death, but when or how soon will that spiritual review occur? This question cannot be answered without examining the relative nature of time in its various forms, "One day is with the Lord as a thousand years, and a thousand years as one day (2 Peter 3:8)," and "For a thousand years in thy sight are but as yesterday when it is past, and as a watch in the night (Psalms 90:4)."

So, what is the true nature of time if our human estimation does not match God's? Today, science struggles with the very same conundrum of identifying time. Obviously, time is not exactly the same for every observer because of a different frame of reference, but for our discussion, time can be divided into three basic categories: Individual Time, Cosmic Time, and God's Time which we will momentarily call Eternity. Notwithstanding, as we will see, there might be more to God's Time of Eternity than initially meets the eye.

Individual Time equates to a person's lifespan - an interval that is unique to every one of us. We all have one, but no two are the same. Despite the difference between each lifetime, God remains the universal constant over all, as King David said, "My times are in thy hand… (Psalms 31:15)."

Cosmic Time is the duration of this current universe, containing every single lifespan from the Creation until heaven and earth cease to be, "And I saw a great white throne, and him that sat on it, <u>from whose face the earth and the heaven fled away; and there was found no place for them</u> (Revelation 20:11)," or "Lift up your eyes to the heavens, and look upon the earth beneath: for <u>the heavens shall vanish away like smoke, and the earth shall wax old like a garment, and they that dwell therein shall die in like manner</u> (Isaiah 51:6)," and "Of old hast thou laid the foundation of the earth: and the heavens are the work of thy hands. <u>26They shall perish, but thou shalt endure: yea, all of them shall wax old like a garment; as a vesture shalt thou change them, and they shall be changed</u>: <u>27But thou art the same, and thy years shall have no end</u> (Psalms 102:25-27, Hebrews 1:10)." What an amazing metaphor that the reality of this present Cosmic Cycle is nothing more than a change of clothes that God will eventually take off when the garment is threadbare before donning a new ensemble.

The term "God's Time" is used in a very general way, understanding that the Almighty inhabits eternity while not being bound by that interval since He is greater and should not be equated with it. According to David, "Before the mountains were brought forth, or ever you had formed the earth and the world, <u>from everlasting to everlasting you are God</u> (Psalms 90:2)."

But what exactly is eternity in comparison to the Psalmist's statement? Is David talking about "eternity past" and "eternity future" when he refers to "everlasting" to "everlasting," or is he actually saying that multiple eternities can transition from one to the other under God's oversight since He alone is greater than eternity and should not be equated with it? Is David's concept of "everlasting" what we identify as a Cosmic Cycle, a unit that is infinitely long without being infinite since the universe is bound by a beginning and an end, but God is not? Or is "everlasting" truly infinite but divided into past and future with an interruption of Cosmic Time in the middle?

By David's statement, "Before the mountains were brought forth, or ever you had formed the earth and the world…" then our current Cosmic Time did not yet exist to separate "eternity past" from "eternity future." Thus, it would appear that the Psalmist might be suggesting the possibility of multiple eternities… infinitely long periods that are not actually infinite, of which God is greater. Regardless of our definition, let us ask the question three ways, "How many divisions within 'one eternity,' or intervals of 'Cosmic Time,' or 'reoccurring eternities' are represented by David's 'everlasting to everlasting?'"

Before answering that question, it might help to know how many times God has created the Cosmos. Currently, Scripture alludes to two Creations, our current reality (Genesis, chapter 1) and a future New Heaven and New Earth (Isaiah 65:17 & Revelation 21:1). However, if we allow for the existence of two Cosmic Cycles or intervals of Cosmic Time, then why not three? Many people believe Genesis 1:1 might suggest a previous creation that was destroyed in Genesis 1:2, prior to the recreation of our own reality in Genesis 1:3-31. If this is so, then Scripture mentions three Cosmic Cycles or intervals of Cosmic Time, and if three, then why not four... five... ten... one hundred, or a thousand, etc.? If God has created more than once, and we know by Scripture that He either has or will, then what prevents Him from creating again and again and again? Are you aware of any divine law that forbids God from creating multiple times?

If the Bible allows for infinite Cosmic Cycles beyond the two we absolutely know (Genesis 1 and Isaiah 65:17/ Revelation 21:1), then are there any residual vestiges of past Creations that we can identify in Scripture? Possibly!

Jesus said that after death, humans will be the same as the angels, "Neither can they die any more: <u>for they are equal unto the angels</u>; and are the children of God, being the children of the resurrection (Luke 20:36)." Consequently, if after death and the resurrection, we become the same as angels ("equal unto the angels") then where did angels come from and when did they first appear in their myriad of forms [Ezekiel 1:5–11, Ezekiel 10:14 (Cherubim), Isaiah 6:1–8 (Seraphim – fiery serpent), Revelation 12:9 (serpent/dragon)]? Did the angels also become the "Sons of God" subsequent to a cycle of ancient resurrections, akin to Jesus' promise for humanity? Could angels be the redeemed remnants of previous creations, as we will become after this universe ends and before the next cosmos begins?

To answer that question, we must know the time of the angels' creation!

If angels were not redeemed from some other previous cosmic cycle, then when in our current time were they formed? Obviously, angels were not made at any time during the Six Days of Creation in Genesis 1, "In the beginning God (Elohim) created the heavens and the earth (Genesis 1:1)." In fact, when Elohim (the plural form of God) discussed mankind's creation, the Bible says, "And God (Elohim) said, Let us make man in our image, after our likeness: and let them have dominion over the fish of the sea, and over the fowl of the air, and over the cattle, and over all the earth, and over every creeping thing that creepeth upon the earth (Genesis 1:26)."

Some believe the plural form of God "Elohim" and the pronouns "us" and "our," refer to the triune godhead - the trinity. Other people believe that God is speaking to His council of angels… the same council mentioned by Asaph in Psalms 82:1-8, "God standeth in the <u>congregation of the mighty; he judgeth among the gods</u>. 2How long will ye judge unjustly, and accept the persons of the wicked? Selah. 3Defend the poor and fatherless: do justice to the afflicted and needy. 4Deliver the poor and needy: rid them out of the hand of the wicked. 5They know not, neither will they understand; they walk on in darkness: all the foundations of the earth are out of course. 6<u>I have said, Ye are gods; and all of you are children of the most High</u>. 7But ye shall die like men, and fall like one of the princes. 8Arise, O God, judge the earth: for thou shalt inherit all nations."

In the above text, we see God addressing a congregation of mighty demigods (angels) who have done a very poor job of administering earthly affairs placed under their control. Consequently, the Almighty reprimands the group of angels that failed to oversee His Creation for the wellbeing of mankind. He warns these demigods (angels) that they will die "like men" if their performance does not improve. By using the words "like men," we realize that a clear distinction exists between the demigods and mankind. Although both might perish as a penalty for sin, yet the two groups are not the same or the simile "like men" would not have been used.

This same Council of Angels existed prior to our cosmos when God's Sons all joined in celebrating the beginning of the present creation that they obviously predated. Listen to the question that God asked Job, "Where wast thou when I laid the foundations of the earth? declare, if thou hast understanding. 5Who hath laid the measures thereof, if thou knowest? or who hath stretched the line upon it? 6Whereupon are the foundations thereof fastened? or who laid the corner stone thereof; <u>7When the 'morning stars' (metaphor for angels) sang together, and all the 'sons of God' (Old Testament reference to angels) shouted for joy</u>? (Job 38:4-7)." Although Job was not alive at the time of Creation and was ignorant of any details, yet the angels were already present as witnesses to God's manifest glory and celebrated His marvelous work.

If the angels predated this current cosmic cycle, then have they always been pre-existent with God? No, unquestionably not! They are created beings just as we are, but their genesis simply predates ours. Ezekiel 28:13-15 chronicles the creation of one angel who was in Eden at the beginning and also in the Mountain of God (Heaven) but later fell from favor, "<u>Thou hast been in Eden the garden of God</u>; every precious stone was thy covering, the sardius, topaz, and the diamond, the beryl, the onyx, and the jasper, the sapphire, the emerald, and the carbuncle, and gold: the workmanship of thy tabrets and of thy pipes <u>was prepared in thee in the day that thou wast created. 14Thou art the anointed cherub that covereth; and I have set thee so: thou wast upon the holy mountain of God; thou hast walked up and down in the midst of the stones of fire.</u> 15Thou wast perfect in thy ways <u>from the day that thou wast created</u>, till iniquity was found in thee." Without knowing the exact moment of their birth, the passage suggests that angels resulted from a previous ancient creation and were then brought forward into our current Cosmic Cycle, just as redeemed humanity will be included in the future New Heaven and New Earth when Jesus said that we would be "equal unto the angels; and are the children of God, being the children of the resurrection (Luke 20:36)."

Impossible to absolutely solve, the mystery's purpose is meant to highlight the complex nature of time which complicates our understanding of what occurs immediately after death. We know that judgment must follow death, but how soon afterwards? Until the resurrection and the judgment occur, where exactly do we go "to be present with the Lord (2 Corinthians 5:8)," and how long do we stay in that location?

CHAPTER TWO

JUDGMENT

Without knowing the interval between, we have already established that death is followed by judgment (after the resurrection), but which judgment is actually involved since there might be more than one?

In the Gospels, Jesus often spoke of judgment to illustrate eternal rewards.

In Matthew 13:24-30, Christ taught the lesson about the tares, "The kingdom of heaven is likened unto a man which sowed good seed in his field: 25But while men slept, his enemy came and sowed tares among the wheat, and went his way. 26But when the blade was sprung up, and brought forth fruit, then appeared the tares also. 27So the servants of the householder came and said unto him, Sir, didst not thou sow good seed in thy field? from whence then hath it tares? 28He said unto them, An enemy hath done this. The servants said unto him, Wilt thou then that we go and gather them up? 29But he said, Nay; lest while ye gather up the tares, ye root up also the wheat with them. 30Let both grow together until the harvest: and in the time of harvest I will say to the reapers, Gather ye together first the tares, and bind them in bundles to burn them: but gather the wheat into my barn." In summary, we notice a harvest in which the bad are burned but the good are stored in a barn when the final judgment occurs.

In Matthew 25:31-41, we read the parable about the sheep and the goats, "When the Son of man shall come in his glory, and all the holy angels with him, then shall he sit upon the throne of his glory: 32And before him shall be gathered all nations: <u>and he shall separate them one from another, as a shepherd divideth his sheep from the goats: 33And he shall set the sheep on his right hand, but the goats on the left</u>. 34Then shall the King say unto them on his right hand, <u>Come, ye blessed of my Father, inherit the kingdom prepared for you from the foundation of the world...</u> 41Then shall he say also unto them on the left hand, <u>Depart from me, ye cursed, into everlasting fire, prepared for the devil and his angels.</u>" When Jesus spoke of His return at the Last Day, He promised to divide the nations right and left, based on the way individuals treated their neighbors and then reward them accordingly.

Another place in the New Testament, Jesus told a story about a group of servants who were entrusted with their master's estate, "For the kingdom of heaven is as a man traveling into a far country, who called his own servants, and delivered unto them his goods... <u>19After a long time the lord of those servants cometh, and reckoneth with them</u> (Matthew 25:14-19)."

The landlord returned after a lengthy absence and began

counting the profits from the investments his stewards made. He found that several had done well with what they were given in the beginning, but one lazy worker did not even try. Consequently, the owner of the estate rebuked him harshly, "His lord answered and said unto him, Thou wicked and slothful servant, thou knewest that I reap where I sowed not, and gather where I have not strawed (Matthew 25:26)."

After the accounting was finished, then each servant was rewarded accordingly, "For unto every one that hath shall be given, and he shall have abundance: but from him that hath not shall be taken away even that which he hath. 30And cast ye the unprofitable servant into outer darkness: there shall be weeping and gnashing of teeth (Matthew 25:29-30)." In the end, we witness the outcome of judgment.

While commending a gentile for having faith, Christ contrasted those who were born to God's promise but refused to believe, "When Jesus heard it, he marveled, and said to them that followed, Verily I say unto you, I have not found so great faith, no, not in Israel. 11And I say unto you, That many shall come from the east and west, and shall sit down with Abraham, and Isaac, and Jacob, in the kingdom of heaven. 12But the children of the kingdom shall be cast out into outer darkness: there shall be weeping and gnashing of teeth (Matthew 8:10-12)." Once again, we notice that the judgment and assignment of rewards are scheduled for the end of time when believers are gathered into God's

Kingdom with Abraham, Isaac, and Jacob who currently wait to be resurrected from the dead.

Even more important, Jesus added an extra detail in Matthew 23:15, "Woe unto you, scribes and Pharisees, hypocrites! for ye compass sea and land to make one proselyte, and when he is made, ye make him twofold more the child of hell than yourselves." And again, "If thy hand offend thee, cut it off: it is better for thee to enter into life maimed, than having two hands to go into hell, into the fire that never shall be quenched (Mark 9:43)." Finally, "I will forewarn you whom ye shall fear: Fear him, which after he hath killed hath power to cast into hell; yea, I say unto you, Fear him (Luke 12:5)."

In all three verses, Christ makes reference to hell. Whether in the Old Testament or the New Testament, the Hebrew word "Sheol" or the Greek word "Hades" is most often translated "Hell" in our early English Bibles since the ordinary residence of the dead was called "Helle" in Old Frisian, "Hel" in Old Norse, "Hölle" in Germanic, and "Halja" in the Gothic – all contributing languages to modern English. Although the early translation of Hell meant the "dwelling place of the dead," the term has gradually changed in modern theology to represent eternal torment after the final judgment when individuals suffer for their sins. This misnomer will be discussed more in Chapter Three; however, we must note in Matthew 23:15, Mark 9:43, and Luke 12:5 that Jesus originally used a different word than Sheol, Hades, or Hell to identify the place of eternal torment following the final judgment – Gehenna!

Gehenna, or the Valley of Hinnom, is referenced a total of twelve times in the New Testament (eleven times by Jesus) and is misnamed "Hell" in early English translations. Gehenna was located outside Jerusalem's wall and served as the city dump where trash was constantly burned. Also known as Tophet, or the valley of dead bones, Christ used the location as a metaphor to describe the Lake of Fire where sinners will be cast after the White Throne Judgment, "And whosoever was not found written in the book of life <u>was cast into the lake of fire</u> (Revelation 20:15)."

The prophet Isaiah also used the analogy of "Gehenna - the Valley of Hinnom" when describing the events after our universe is destroyed at the End of Time, "<u>For as the new heavens and the new earth, which I will make, shall remain before me</u>, saith the LORD, so shall your seed and your name remain. 23And it shall come to pass, that from one new moon to another, and from one sabbath to another, shall all flesh come to worship before me, saith the LORD. <u>24And they shall go forth (outside the city), and look upon the carcases of the men that have transgressed against me: for their worm shall not die, neither shall their fire be quenched; and they shall be an abhorring unto all flesh</u> (Isaiah 66:22-24)."

John utilized the same comparison when describing New Jerusalem that will appear after the next cosmos is created,

"Blessed are they that do his commandments, that they may have right to the tree of life, and may enter in through the gates into the city (New Jerusalem). <u>15For without (outside the city) are dogs, and sorcerers, and whoremongers, and murderers, and idolaters, and whosoever loveth and maketh a lie</u> (Revelation 22:14-15)." After judgment, we again see that the wicked are consigned to a place of torment beyond the city wall – the trash dump of Gehenna, the Valley of Hinnom… the eternal Lake of Fire (that should not be confused with the present abode of the dead – Sheol, Hades, or Hell which we will exhaustively examine later).

Revisiting 2 Corinthians 5:10, St. Paul confirms, "For we must all appear before the judgment seat of Christ; that every one may receive the things done in his body, according to that he hath done, whether it be good or bad."

Currently, the prevailing opinion in Western Christianity is that the Judgment Seat of Christ specifically pertains to the Church after the First Resurrection, "<u>And I saw thrones, and they sat on them, and judgment was committed to them</u>. Then I saw the souls of those who had been beheaded for their witness to Jesus and for the word of God, who had not worshiped the beast or his image, and had not received his mark on their foreheads or on their hands. <u>And they lived and reigned with Christ for a thousand years. 5But the rest of the dead did not live again until the thousand years were finished. This is the first resurrection</u> (Revelation 20:4-5)."

But in Revelation 20:11-14, another judgment is portrayed that many believe will occur after the Judgment Seat of Christ, "<u>And I saw a great white throne, and him that sat on it, from whose face the earth and the heaven fled away; and there was found no place for them</u>. 12And I saw the dead, small and great, stand before God; <u>and the books were opened: and another book was opened, which is the book of life: and the dead were judged out of those things which were written in the books, according to their works</u>. 13And the sea gave up the dead which were in it; and death and hell delivered up the dead which were in them: <u>and they were judged every man according to their works. 14And death and hell were cast into the lake of fire. This is the second death</u>."

However, the Medieval Church and the early Reformers did not teach two separate judgments for believers and sinners raised from the dead during the First and Second Resurrection since "Amillennialists" refused to accept the dispensation of Christ's Earthly Kingdom that appears before the destruction of our cosmos. Instead, they viewed the Church Age as the Kingdom Age of Christ and the Great White Throne as the one and only judgment at the end of time when the heavens and earth are scheduled to be destroyed. For the Amillennialists, the Judgment Seat of Christ is the same as the White Throne Judgment. I have my opinion, but regardless of what we believe about Amillennialism or Dispensationalism, the conflict between the two doctrines does not interfere with our discussion of what occurs at the end of life. Either way, the dead will eventually be judged following the resurrection whether their evaluation is the Judgment Seat of Christ or the Great White Throne. The main point is that judgment does not occur instantly after death which requires a holding area for the soul until the resurrection when we will be judged to receive our final rewards, good or bad.

After exploring Jesus' use of the word "Gehenna" to represent final banishment to the Lake of Fire, we should wonder what criterion determines the verdict for eternal damnation. The answer is found in Revelation 20:12-13 & 15, "And I saw the dead, small and great, stand before God; and the books were opened: and another book was opened, which is the book of life: and the dead were judged out of those things which were written in the books, according to their works. 13And the sea gave up the dead which were in it; and death and hell delivered up the dead which were in them: and they were judged every man according to their works. 15And whosoever was not found written in the book of life was cast into the lake of fire."

Besides a review of our earthly works, the primary consideration is based on names being written in the Book of Life. Regardless of what we have done whether good or bad, if our names are not listed in the Book of Life, then the omission mandates automatic disqualification and condemnation.

Here is a tantalizing mystery!

Supporting the doctrine of hyper-Calvinism, numerous Scriptures declare that the Elect Believers were chosen in Christ before this Creation ever began, "According as he hath chosen us in him before the foundation of the world, that we should be holy and without blame before him in love: 5Having predestinated us unto the adoption of children by Jesus Christ to himself, according to the good pleasure of his will (Ephesians 1:4-5)."

Already chosen to be God's Elect, our names were written in THE BOOK before this world was formed, "The beast that thou sawest was, and is not; and shall ascend out of the bottomless pit, and go into perdition: and they that dwell on the earth shall wonder, whose names were not written in the book of life from the foundation of the world, when they behold the beast that was, and is not, and yet is (Revelation 17:8)."

David said virtually the same thing about being written in God's Book before life started, "Thine eyes did see my substance, yet being unperfect; and in thy book all my members were written, which in continuance were fashioned, when as yet there was none of them (Psalms 139:16)."

Not only were we already chosen, but Christ was also slain before the Creation, "And all that dwell upon the earth shall worship him (Antichrist), whose names are not written in the book of life of the Lamb slain from the foundation of the world (Revelation 13:8)." Thus, our selection to be saved and Christ's divine mission to be crucified were both pre-existent in THE BOOK before reality began. It was a done deal!

Nevertheless, there is an odd twist about the names being recorded in the Book of Life. Consider Moses' prayer while he mediated as an intercessor for Israel, "Yet now, if thou wilt forgive their sin; and if not, <u>blot me, I pray thee, out of thy book which thou hast written</u> (Exodus 32:32)."

Often ignored, names can be blotted out of the Book of Life, "<u>Let them be blotted out of the book of the living</u>, and not be written with the righteous (Psalms 69:28)," or "He that overcometh, the same shall be clothed in white raiment; and <u>I will not blot out his name out of the book of life</u>, but I will confess his name before my Father, and before his angels (Revelation 3:5)," and finally, "If any man shall take away from the words of the book of this prophecy, <u>God shall take away his part out of the book of life</u>, and out of the holy city, and from the things which are written in this book (Revelation 22:19)." However, nowhere in Scripture do we ever find names added to the Book of Life if they were not already there before the Cosmos came into being.

Suddenly, we understand exactly what Jesus meant when He said, "And then will I profess unto them, <u>I never knew you</u>: depart from me, ye that work iniquity (Matthew 7:23)," and "I tell you, <u>I know you not whence ye are</u>; depart from me, all ye workers of iniquity (Luke 13:27." Christ was not exaggerating or speaking an untruth when He said, "I have no idea who you are!" If the person's name was not recorded in the Book of Life from the beginning of time, or if the name had been blotted out during the person's lifetime, then the individual literally disappeared from the mind of God as if they had never lived.

Returning to what we noticed before… After our present reality ends, the people who enter the New Creation must have their names already written in the Book of Life, "Then I saw a great white throne and him who was seated on it. The earth and the heavens fled from his presence, and there was no place for them (This world ceases to be - Isaiah 51:6) 15Anyone whose name was not found written in the book of life was thrown into the lake of fire (Rev. 20:11&15)."

Thus, if God's Chosen were already written in the BOOK before this world began and if they are the only individuals going into the New Creation because their names are recorded in the very same BOOK, then does that make them Cosmic Travelers who were predestined before either this Creation or the one to come? If so, then how many cosmic cycles have the Elect experienced? How many times have they been "sent and re-gathered?"

The above possibility reminds me of our earlier discussion about the angels who were made during some previous cosmic cycle to be included in this Creation for the purpose of fulfilling God's will, just as Jesus promised that we will ultimately be "equal to the angels" as Sons of God and Children of the Resurrection. Is it merely my hyper-Calvinism speaking, or does this scenario seem like a long-running simulation on a universal scale?

Without any memory of a previous existence in an earlier creation, is there a trail of breadcrumbs that leaves clues other than having our names written in God's Book prior to the formation of this earth? Possibly, but the evidence must be in Scripture alone. King Solomon, the wisest and most knowledgeable of men, said that after we die, "then shall the dust return to the earth as it was: and <u>the spirit shall return unto God who gave it</u> (Ecclesiastes 12:7)."

In the previous verse, Solomon wrote "return" twice. The original Hebrew word being used is "šûḇ / shoob," to bring back, allow to return, put back, draw back, give back, restore. According to the writer… the human body resorts to its original state after life ends, "And the LORD God formed man of the dust of the ground (Genesis 2:7)." In spite of being recorded in God's Book before the Creation, our bodies waited for the planet to form before arising from the dirt, and to the dirt we will ultimately return.

However, the body is only half of our being. Consequently, Moses' account continues in Genesis 2:7, "And (God) breathed into his (humanity's) nostrils the <u>breath of life</u> (the Neshama); and man became a <u>living soul</u> (nefesh – person or mind)." While the body returns to dust at death, our ethereal entity goes back to God from whom it sprang before the Beginning. Much like Jesus who was the Logos (the creative expression of the Word), we had an earlier presence/existence with God that was only later "made flesh (John 1:14)."

Regarding our lack of memory from a previous "state of being," there is a mystifying story in Jewish tradition that explains the philtrum - the groove on the upper lip. In the Midrash (Tanhuma Pekudei 3), a female angel named Lailah is the instructor of every human before they are born. She lights a candle and shows each soul the entirety of earth and then teaches their spirit all of God's Law. However, when the time comes for birth, Lailah touches the child's upper lip to say, "Shhh..." and the baby forgets everything it heard in order to learn again during life through experience.

Oddly, this same general idea was proposed by Carl Jung, an adamant supporter of Sigmund Freud. An active member of the Vienna Psychoanalytic Society, Jung believed that thoughts, connections, behaviors, and feelings all innately exist in each of us and manifest themselves as a sense of belonging, love, fear, etc., that makes up our instinctive "collective unconscious." We know, even though we don't know that we know, and according to Jewish tradition, this is the work of the angel Lailah who accompanies individual souls from one world to the next.

What an amazing conundrum, but we cannot stop here because Paradise awaits!

CHAPTER THREE

PARADISE

Earlier we introduced the Hebrew "Sheol" and the Greek "Hades" as ancient names of a repository for the dead which was translated by early English Bibles into the word "Hell" and has been more recently confused with "Gehenna - the Lake of Fire" following the White Throne Judgment. Despite the mix-up, how can we demonstrate that Hell is not the Lake of Fire? The proof is very easy if we refer to the passage that describes the White Throne Judgment after the current Creation ends.

Ponder this verse for a moment, "And <u>death and hell were cast into the lake of fire</u>. This is the second death (Revelation 20:14)."

In the parent Greek, the original word for "Hell" was "Hades," a place for disembodied spirits. Thus, between the destruction of this Cosmos and the appearance of the New Creation, the Realm of the Dead will be cast into the Lake of Fire which depicts the "death of death," i.e., the Second Death.

Now, consider the English translation of a Hebrew text, "For thou wilt not leave my soul in hell; neither wilt thou suffer thine Holy One to see corruption (Psalms 16:10)."

This passage is a prophetic reference to Christ's resurrection on the third day, prior to the Jewish day of corruption on day four when Martha spoke of her brother Lazarus, "By now he stinketh (John 11:39)." In Psalms 16:10, David rejoiced because Christ would be resurrected before corruption on the fourth day, and he (David) would be rescued from Hell. But the English "Hell" is the Hebrew "Sheol" comparable to the Greek "Hades" which will be cast into the Lake of Fire ahead of the New Creation! Consequently, Hell cannot be the Lake of Fire… since Hell is destined to be cast into the Lake of Fire. One cannot be the other! Instead, Sheol, Hades, and Hell represent the grave or the abode of the dead. Thus, death and the grave will be cast into the Lake of Fire, along with everyone who is not written in the Book of Life.

Although Sheol, Hades, and Hell were often portrayed as gloomy somber places, a different holding area for disembodied spirits is very beautiful and often misidentified as the realm where God lives; however, Paradise and Heaven are not exactly the same, as we will see.

Before we search the Scripture, let's explore how the Early Church Fathers viewed Paradise.

According to Irenaeus (circa 180 A.D.), "In paradise certainly, as the Scripture declares, 'And God planted a garden [paradisum] eastward in Eden, and there He placed the man whom He had formed.' And then afterwards when [man] proved disobedient, he was cast out thence into this world. <u>Wherefore also the elders who were disciples of the apostles tell us that those who were *translated were transferred to that place (for paradise has been prepared for righteous men, such as have the Spirit; in which place also Paul the apostle, when he was caught up, heard words which are unspeakable as regards us in our present condition), and that there shall they who have been *translated remain until the Consummation [of all things], as a prelude to immortality.</u>" *NOTE: Irenaeus used the word "translated" for those who died and also mentioned that our immortality does not begin until after the Consummation (Judgment).

So, according to Irenaeus, Paradise was created for mankind, but after Adam and Eve's sin and banishment, God translated/sent the righteous dead back to Paradise until the completion of all things. We have already identified the Consummation as the judgment that follows the resurrection before the New Heaven and New Earth are formed. Irenaeus used St. Paul as an example of a believer who was translated to Paradise (during a near-death experience). Later, we will provide scriptural support for Irenaeus' claim.

Another early Church Father named Theophilus (180 A.D.) said, "For man had been made a middle nature, neither wholly mortal, nor altogether immortal, but capable of either; <u>so also the place, Paradise, was made in respect of beauty intermediate between earth and heaven</u>." Theophilus believed that Paradise was the middle ground between

Heaven and Earth, more divine than our natural world but less perfect than God's abode.

Akin to Sheol, Hades, and Hell... Paradise is a temporary residence for the dead until they can be judged prior to the next creation cycle. We know this is true because of something Christ said during His crucifixion. Hanging nearby, one of the dying thieves pleaded, "...Lord, remember me when thou comest into thy kingdom. 43And Jesus said unto him, Verily I say unto thee, <u>Today shalt thou be with me in paradise</u> (Luke 23:42-43)." Momentarily, we will examine a mystery created by this promise.

Paradise was another term similar to the Jewish Sheol and the Greek Hades, figuratively referenced as Abraham's Bosom in the parable of Lazarus, "And it came to pass, that the beggar died, and was carried by the angels <u>into Abraham's bosom</u>: the rich man also died, and was buried; 23<u>And in hell</u> he lift up his eyes, being in torments, <u>and seeth Abraham afar off, and Lazarus in his bosom</u> (Luke 16:22-23)."

Comparable to Abraham's Bosom... Paradise was undoubtedly the place of rest for the Prophet Samuel who was disturbed by King Saul, "And Samuel said to Saul, Why hast thou <u>disquieted</u> (disturbed) me, to <u>bring me up</u>? And Saul answered, I am sore distressed; for the Philistines make war against me, and God is departed from me, and answereth me no more, neither by prophets, nor by dreams:

therefore I have called thee, that thou mayest make known unto me what I shall do (1 Samuel 28:15)."

According to the Early Church Fathers… Paradise was Adam and Eve's original home that contained the Tree of Life - from which they were expelled following their sin which led to death, "In paradise certainly, as the Scripture declares, 'And God planted a garden [paradisum] eastward in Eden, and there He placed the man whom He had formed.' And then afterwards when [man] proved disobedient, he was cast out thence into this world (Irenaeus - circa 180 A.D.)."

Interestingly, notice that Irenaeus viewed the world as being totally separated from Paradise where mankind began, which suggests that the early Church Fathers didn't view God's supernatural garden as being part of the natural creation on this planet. Much like the angels who fell from their first estate in Heaven, so did we!

However, when Jesus promised to join the thief in Paradise before the day ended, the assurance seemed to create a conflict regarding another destination where the Lord's spirit would go during his three-day burial in the tomb. Notice what St. Paul said, "But unto every one of us is given grace according to the measure of the gift of Christ. 8Wherefore he saith, When he ascended up on high, he led captivity captive, and gave gifts unto men. 9Now that he ascended, what is it but that he also descended first into the lower parts of the earth? 10He that descended is the same also that ascended up far above 'all heavens' (plural), that he might fill all things (Ephesians 4:7-10)." According to the Apostle, before Jesus ascended above "all heavens," He first descended into the depths of Sheol or Hell, but for what purpose?

This time, we examine the doctrine of St. Peter, "For Christ also hath once suffered for sins, the just for the unjust, that he might bring us to God, being put to death in the flesh, but quickened by the Spirit: 19By which also he went and preached unto the spirits in prison; 20Which sometime were disobedient, when once the longsuffering of God waited in the days of Noah, while the ark was a preparing, wherein few, that is, eight souls were saved by water (1 Peter 3:18-20)."

Prefigured by the Messianic prophecy of Isaiah 61:1, "The Spirit of the Lord GOD is upon me; because the LORD hath anointed me to preach good tidings unto the meek; he hath sent me to bind up the brokenhearted, to proclaim liberty to the captives, and the opening of the prison to them that are bound (Isaiah 61:1)," Peter explained that Jesus went into Hell and preached the Gospel. Some theologians try to rationalize that Christ went to the righteous Old Testament saints languishing in Sheol to prove that God's prophecy of salvation was finally fulfilled. However, the Apostle clearly stated that Jesus' audience was comprised of "disobedient spirits" that were imprisoned in Noah's day when the ancient flood destroyed mankind, which makes sense since St. Paul said that Jesus descended into Sheol/Hell to "lead captivity captive and give gifts unto men."

But here's the problem, if Jesus promised to join the dying thief in glorious Paradise, how could the Savior also be in gloomy Hell preaching the message of salvation to the damned? To answer that question, we must know the location of both Paradise and Hell, but can we find them? Absolutely, but we must return to a verse already mentioned, "And it came to pass, that the beggar died, and was carried by the angels into Abraham's bosom (Paradise): the rich man also died, and was buried; 23And in hell he lift up his eyes, being in torments, and seeth Abraham afar off, and Lazarus in his bosom (Luke 16:22-23)."

According to Christ's parable about "Poor Lazarus and the Rich Man," Paradise (Abraham's bosom) and Sheol (Hell) exist in the same spiritual plane/dimension despite the chasm separating them, "...between us and you there is a great gulf fixed: so that they which would pass from hence to you cannot; neither can they pass to us, that would come from thence (Luke 16:26)." How do we know that Paradise and Hell are located in the same place? Because both are clearly visible to each other since the Rich Man could see Lazarus.

The likelihood that the residence of the dead (Paradise and Sheol/Hell) both occupy the same spiritual realm is confirmed by an ancient document commonly read by both Jews and Christians of the 1st Century. How do we know?

Because fragments of the scroll were found in the Qumran Caves between 1947 and 1956.

Although I am fascinated with the books of 1 and 2 Enoch, yet I do not quote them authoritatively since they were not included in our biblical canon after the Church Council of Laodicea (364), Hippo (393), and Carthage (397). However, for our purposes here, we will examine what 2 Enoch says about the location of Paradise merely as an ancient source and then move on to a scriptural parallel.

According to the Bible, "...Enoch walked with God: and he was not; for God took him (Genesis 5:24)." Tradition tells us that after Enoch had walked with God and before he was taken the final time, the man left an account of his spiritual travels with his great-grandson Noah. As Enoch was guided through progressively higher levels of Heaven, he carefully noted what he saw. Arriving at the Third Heaven, the man witnessed Paradise in the eighth chapter of 2 Enoch, "And paradise is in between the corruptible and the incorruptible. And two streams come forth, one a source of honey and milk, and a source which produces oil and wine. And it is divided into four parts, and they go around with a quiet movement. And they come out into the paradise of Eden, between the corruptible and the incorruptible." According to 2 Enoch, this realm was in the 3rd of 10 levels of Heaven. Enoch stated that the 10th Heaven was where God lived.

First of all, can we prove that Heaven is divided into different levels or dimensions? Yes, refer back to St.

Paul's statement about Christ's ministry in Hell, "<u>He that descended is the same also that ascended up far above ALL HEAVENS,</u> that he might fill all things (Ephesians 4:10)." The allusion to "all Heavens" implies a multitude. As we proceed, we will also discover other references to various heavenly levels or realms.

However, while Enoch was visiting Paradise in the third part of Heaven (Chapter 9), he spied another home for the dead that occupied the same spiritual dimension – Hell (Chapter 10), "And those two men led me up on to the Northern side, and showed me there a very terrible place, and (there were) all manner of tortures in that place: cruel darkness and unillumined gloom, and there is no light there, but murky fire constantly flaming aloft, and (there is) a fiery river coming forth, and that whole place is everywhere fire, and everywhere (there is) frost and ice, thirst and shivering, while the bonds are very cruel, and the angels (spirits) fearful and merciless, bearing angry weapons, merciless torture (2 Enoch 10:1)."

Alarmed by the great difference between the two partitions of the Third Heaven, Enoch exclaimed, "Woe, woe, how very terrible is this place (2 Enoch 10:2)!"

Surprisingly, Enoch provided a list of extreme sins that distinguished the residents of Hell from the disembodied souls that inhabited Paradise although both were located in the same spiritual plane, "And those men said to me: This place, O Enoch, is prepared for those who dishonour God, who on earth practice sin against nature, which is child-corruption after the sodomitic fashion, magic-making, enchantments and devilish witchcrafts, and who boast of their wicked deeds, stealing, lies, calumnies, envy, rancour, fornication, murder, and who, accursed, steal the souls of men, who, seeing the poor take away their goods and themselves wax rich, injuring them for other men's goods; who being able to satisfy the empty, made the hungering to die (the rich man's sin against poor Lazarus); being able to clothe, stripped the naked; and who knew not their creator, and bowed to the soulless (and lifeless) gods, who cannot see nor hear, vain gods, (who also) built hewn images and bow down to unclean handiwork, for all these is prepared this place among these... (2 Enoch 10:3)."

Reiterating, I do not quote 2 Enoch authoritatively since the Church did not include the book in our official canon but use the ancient document merely to identify parallels with our Holy Bible.

Regardless of credibility for Enoch's account, did you realize that an apostle said virtually the same thing about the location of Paradise?

When St. Paul passed through the city of Lystra, a group of rabble-rousers instigated a mob for stoning him to death, "And there came thither (to Lystra – vs 8) certain Jews from Antioch and Iconium, who persuaded the people, and, <u>having stoned Paul, drew him out of the city, supposing he had been dead</u> (Acts 14:19)."

Amazingly, when the believers prayed over the apostle's dead body, the man came back to life, "Howbeit, as the disciples stood round about him, he rose up, and came into the city: and the next day he departed with Barnabas to Derbe (Acts 14:20)."

Can we be sure that Paul was dead? Most likely, due to the near-death experience that he described later, "I know a man in Christ (St. Paul modestly referred to himself) who fourteen years ago was <u>caught up to the THIRD HEAVEN</u>. Whether it was in the body (alive) or out of the body (dead) I do not know--God knows (2 Corinthians 12:2)."

And the story continues, "How that he was caught up into PARADISE, and heard unspeakable words, which it is not lawful for a man to utter (2 Corinthians 12:4)."

Thus, St. Paul provided the smoking gun for identifying the EXACT location of Paradise... in the Third Heaven where Enoch also visited Hell!

This is EXACTLY what the Early Church Fathers believed, but we have drifted away from that original doctrine with our current fairytale theology that is unsubstantiated by Scripture!

So, let me ask again, "Where do we go after death?"

The answer: We either go to Paradise or Hell - the temporary homes of the dead that continue to exist in the Third Heaven until the conclusion of this present Cosmos at the White Throne Judgment when a BIG CHANGE will occur!

Talking about a big change, I have a question that might end with a shocking revelation, "Can non-Christians go to Paradise?"

Amazingly, that might be a possibility based on one of Jesus' parables; however, time spent in Paradise for good behavior does not mean that a non-Christian will enter God's next creation of the New Heaven and New Earth. That is an impossible prospect without having the person's name written in the Book of Life before this world was ever formed. Let me explain.

Very carefully, let us read one of Jesus' parables about the great feast that God will prepare at the End of Time, "So those servants went out into the highways, and gathered together all as many as they found, <u>both bad and good</u>: and the wedding was furnished with guests (Matthew 22:10)."

In the parable, do you see that everyone "good and bad" was initially gathered to the meal set by God? So often in "near-death experiences" we hear various individuals describe an unimaginably beautiful place filled with peace, love, and light... but mostly unfathomable, immeasurable LOVE! Undoubtedly, they have entered Paradise where everyone temporarily feels the magnitude of God's love that was prepared for us "in Christ Jesus" whether we were good or bad, "For God so loved the world, that he gave his only begotten Son, that whosoever believeth in him should not perish, but have everlasting life. For God sent not his Son into the world to condemn the world; but that the world through him might be saved... According as he hath chosen us in him before the foundation of the world, that we should be holy and without blame before him in love... God, who is rich in mercy, for his great love wherewith he loved us. Even when we were dead in sins, hath quickened us together with Christ, (by grace ye are saved) and hath raised us up together, and made us sit together in heavenly places in Christ Jesus, that in the ages to come he might shew the exceeding riches of his grace in his kindness toward us through Christ Jesus (John 3:16-17, Ephesians 1:4, Ephesians 2:4-7)."

Unfortunately, the story does not end with either the feast or Paradise.

Let us continue with Jesus' parable, "And when the king came in to see the guests (at the feast), he saw there a man which had not on a wedding garment (Believers who are baptized in Christ have literally 'put on Christ!'- Galatians 3:27). And he (the King) saith unto him, Friend, how camest thou in hither not having a wedding garment? And he was speechless (Matthew 22:11)." Here is an example of a non-Christian in Paradise, who joined the feast without making any spiritual preparation in life for what would occur after death.

Let's see what Christ will do, "Then said the king to the servants, Bind him hand and foot, and take him away, and cast him into outer darkness; there shall be weeping and gnashing of teeth. 14For many are called, but few are chosen (Matthew 22:13-14)." Although the person entered Paradise (the feast) after being called away from their time on earth, yet that was no guarantee they were selected to escape the Lake of Fire after Final Judgment without having their name written in the Book of Life.

Thus, according to Jesus' parable, everyone "good and bad" at first entered the glorious feast (Paradise), but after basking in the infinite magnitude of God's love, the guests who did not accept Christ during life were later cast out of the joyous celebration into utter and absolute Darkness filled with screaming and the grinding of teeth. Can you sense the infinite horror of Final Damnation after coming so close to God (in death) to actually feel the love He prepared for us "through Christ Jesus," only to be banished later in the Lake of Fire for rejecting the love that we could have received during our lifetime? That, my friend, will be worse than any Hell you can imagine!

Don't wait! Accept Christ now! "For he saith: In an accepted time have I heard thee; and in the day of salvation have I helped thee. Behold, now is the acceptable time; behold, now is the day of salvation (2 Corinthians 6:2)."

CHAPTER FOUR

RESURRECTION FROM DEATH SLEEP

The Third Heaven is partitioned as a holding area for the departed. Paradise is the happy side for the good (2 Enoch 9, 2 Corinthians 12:2-4); and Hell is the unhappy side for the bad (2 Enoch 10)... but both are self-contained in the same spiritual dimension, which matches Jesus' parable about the rich man and Lazarus! So, by returning to the ancient theology of the Early Church, we have answered a haunting question that currently plagues many people!

Much like anyone else who recovers from a near-death experience, St. Paul was left with an impairment due to injuries he experienced during his stoning, "And lest I should be exalted above measure <u>through the abundance of the revelations</u> (witnessing Paradise in the Third Heaven), there was given to me <u>a thorn in the flesh</u> (physical ailment/ disability), the messenger of Satan to buffet me, lest I should be exalted above measure. 8For this thing I besought the Lord thrice, that it might depart from me. 9And he said unto me, My grace is sufficient for thee: for my strength is made perfect in weakness. Most gladly therefore will I rather glory in my infirmities, that the power of Christ may rest upon me. 10Therefore I take pleasure in infirmities, in reproaches, in necessities, in persecutions, in distresses for Christ's sake: for when I am weak, then am I strong (2 Corinthians 12:7-10)."

The disability probably involved Paul's vision, "<u>And my temptation (illness/disability) which was in my flesh ye despised not, nor rejected</u>; but received me as an angel of God, even as Christ Jesus. 15Where is then the blessedness ye spake of? for I bear you record, that, if it had been possible, <u>ye would have plucked out your own eyes, and have given them to me</u> (Galatians 4:14-15)."

In the apostle's letter to the Galatians, we realize that St. Paul nearly went blind after the stoning, "Ye see how large a letter (what large letters) I have written unto you with mine own hand (Galatians 6:11)!" Although Luke usually wrote Paul's dictation, yet the book of Galatians was personally written by the apostle with very large handwriting that he could see to read.

Similar to most people who visit Paradise during a near-death experience, St. Paul was not afraid to die in the future, "For I am now ready to be offered, and the time of my departure is at hand. 7I have fought a good fight, I have finished my course, I have kept the faith: 8Henceforth there is laid up for me a crown of righteousness, which the Lord, the righteous judge, shall give me at that day: and not to me only, but unto all them also that love his appearing (2 Timothy 4:6-8)."

But what attitude should a Christian have about death, according to Scripture, "And I heard a voice from heaven saying unto me, Write, <u>Blessed (happy) are the dead which die in the Lord</u> from henceforth: Yea, saith the Spirit, that they may rest from their labours; and their works do follow them (Revelation 14:13)?"

What is the Scriptural attitude of God about the death of the righteous, "<u>Precious in the sight of the LORD is the death of his saints.</u> 16O LORD, truly I am thy servant; I am thy servant, and the son of thine handmaid: thou hast loosed my bonds (Ps. 116:15-16)?" Note: In the context of David's previous words, I'm sure his statement "thou hast loosed my bonds" refers to the release of death.

What is the Scriptural attitude of God about the death of the wicked, "Say unto them, As I live, saith the Lord GOD, <u>I have no pleasure in the death of the wicked</u>; but that the wicked turn from his way and live: turn ye, turn ye from your evil ways (Ezekiel 33:11)?"

Finally, what did the early reformers believe about death?

Luther believed in something called "death sleep." Initially, I chafed at the idea, offended that he would not agree with what I was taught, 500 years after the fact. Realizing that many years of "tradition" have been added, I once again returned to Scripture to uncover the early New Testament doctrine of "death sleep," and here is what I found...

"These things said he: and after that he saith unto them, <u>Our friend Lazarus sleepeth</u>; but I go, that I may <u>awake him</u>

out of sleep. 12Then said his disciples, Lord, if he sleep, he shall do well. 13Howbeit Jesus spake of his death: but they thought that he had spoken of taking of rest in sleep (John 11:11-13)."

"For he that eateth and drinketh unworthily, eateth and drinketh damnation to himself, not discerning the Lord's body. 30For this cause many are weak and sickly among you, and many sleep. 31For if we would judge ourselves, we should not be judged (1 Corinthians 11:29-31)."

"After that, he was seen of above five hundred brethren at once; of whom the greater part remain unto this present, but some are fallen asleep (1 Corinthians 15:6)."

"But now is Christ risen from the dead, and become the firstfruits of them that slept (1 Corinthians 15:20)."

"And he kneeled down, and cried with a loud voice, Lord, lay not this sin to their charge. And when he had said this, he fell asleep (Acts 7:60)."

"Behold, I shew you a mystery; We shall not all sleep, but we shall all be changed (1 Corinthians 15:51)."

"But I would not have you to be ignorant, brethren, concerning them which are asleep, that ye sorrow not, even as others which have no hope. 14For if we believe that Jesus died and rose again, even so them also which sleep in Jesus will God bring with him (1 Thessalonians 4:13-14)." Note: To "sleep in Jesus" is to walk through Paradise with God's Son as He walked through the Garden in the cool of the evening with our father Adam (Gen. 3:8).

"And when he was come in, he saith unto them, Why make ye this ado, and weep? the damsel is not dead, <u>but sleepeth</u> (Mark 5:39)."

"And all wept, and bewailed her: but he said, Weep not; <u>she is not dead, but sleepeth</u>. 53And they laughed him to scorn, knowing that she was dead (Luke 8:52-53)."

Now, for a little critical analysis....

If only one person mentioned death sleep or if the concept was mentioned only one time, then we might assume the term was a figurative way of alluding to something unpleasant simply to soften the blow. However, death sleep was repeatedly mentioned by various New Testament authors on many occasions, suggesting a literal doctrine and not a metaphor or allegory.

So, what is the nature of death sleep? To answer that, we must also question the nature of individual reality and awareness which is a truly daunting task. Nevertheless, New Testament death sleep aptly mirrors Old Testament Paradise/Sheol as a place of repose, similar to where Samuel was "resting" in the grave or where Lazarus was "sleeping" in Abraham's Bosom.

Death sleep uniquely parallels Einstein's concept of Relativity based on the observer's position, i.e., death is not the same to the dead as it is to the living.

If someone watches me sleep, then the experience for them is tediously long. However, when I sleep, the transition is instantaneous between the previous evening and the next morning. For a sleeper, the long dark night does not exist unless their rest is disturbed like the Prophet Samuel who rebuked King Saul (1 Samuel 28:15).

Basically, the difference in death for a "living observer" and death for the "dead" involves the riddle of time... lifetime, cosmic time, or eternity. The three are not the same, and their unique identities variously define the nature of death based on relativity. Momentarily gone from this natural realm, the interval might seem like years in Paradise for individuals who are quickly resuscitated. Conversely, at the resurrection, someone who has been dead for eons might only experience their absence as an eternal moment. Cross-dimensional time simply does not relate.

Now, let's return to St. Paul's brave farewell. Before being decapitated by Emperor Nero, the apostle reminded his friend Timothy that a Consummation of the Cosmos was coming, "Henceforth there is laid up for me a crown of righteousness, which the Lord, the righteous judge, shall give me at that day: and not to me only, but unto all them also that love his appearing (2 Timothy 4:8)."

After mentioning the "righteous judge," what "day" did the apostle mean as he eagerly anticipated Jesus' "appearing"? Obviously, Paul spoke of the Consummation of Creation during the White Throne Judgment which also holds an ominous threat for both Paradise and Hell, but we'll consider that dour prospect after first investigating the resurrection.

One of my favorite references to the resurrection comes from the ancient story of Job who probably lived during the days of Abraham. Horribly sick, Job courageously declared, "Oh that my words were now written! oh that they were printed in a book! 24That they were graven with an iron pen and lead in the rock for ever! 25For I know that my redeemer liveth, and that he shall stand at the latter day upon the earth: <u>26And though after my skin worms destroy this body, yet in my flesh shall I see God: 27Whom I shall see for myself, and mine eyes shall behold, and not another; though my reins be consumed within me</u> (Job 19:23-27)."

In great detail, the man clearly described how his sick body would be reconstituted in the Latter Days after maggots left absolutely nothing behind. At the end of time, he would have brand-new eyes filling the empty sockets of his dusty skull to personally see the Redeemer of his natural body instead of merely hearing a rumor while inhabiting the dreary region of Sheol.

Likewise, Solomon used a lovely metaphor in his "Song of Songs" to describe the resurrection, "My beloved is like a roe or a young hart: behold, he standeth behind our wall, he looketh forth at the windows, shewing himself through the lattice. 10My beloved spake, and said unto me, Rise up, my love, my fair one, and come away. 11For, lo, the winter is past, the rain is over and gone; 12The flowers appear on the earth; the time of the singing of birds is come, and the voice of the turtle is heard in our land; 13The fig tree putteth forth her green figs, and the vines with the tender grape give a good smell. Arise, my love, my fair one, and come away (Song of Solomon 2:9-13)."

In Solomon's beguiling song, we recognize the typology of Christ who lovingly watches His followers from afar… through the lattice, as it were. However, after the dreary interim of death ends, He will come at the resurrection like a leaping deer and will take His Church from this present realm to a fresh existence in the next Creation, "Arise, my love, my fair one, and come away!"

Now, notice what Jesus said about the resurrection, "And this is the Father's will which hath sent me, that of all which he hath given me I should lose nothing, but should raise it up again at the last day. 40And this is the will of him that sent me, that every one which seeth the Son, and believeth on him, may have everlasting life: and I will raise him up at the last day…. No man can come to me, except the Father which hath sent me draw him: and I will raise him up at the last day… Whoso eateth my flesh, and drinketh my blood, hath eternal life; and I will raise him up at the last day (John 6:39-40, 44, 54)."

Four times in one conversation, Christ designated that the resurrection would occur at the LAST DAY! If He meant the First Resurrection (prior to the establishment of His earthly kingdom when the Antichrist is destroyed… Dispensationalism), then that "last day" would be when the Mighty Angel, "…sware by him that liveth for ever and ever, who created heaven, and the things that therein are, and the earth, and the things that therein are, and the sea, and the things which are therein, <u>that there should be time no longer</u> (Revelation 10:6)." However, if Jesus instead spoke of the Second Resurrection (that will immediately precede the White Throne Judgment in Revelation 20:11-15... Amillennialism), then the "last day" signals the end of this cosmic cycle and the creation of the New Heaven and New Earth.

I'll let you decide, but either way, one thing is certain; the resurrection and the gathering of Christ's Church will happen at the End of Time and will not be a big secret... as the proponents of John Nelson Darby falsely claim! For your information, John Nelson Darby was an Irish lawyer who became a preacher and promoted a spurious doctrine that Christ's Coming would secretly occur before the Last Days.

Jesus said, "<u>For as the lightning cometh out of the east, and shineth even unto the west</u>; so shall also the coming of the Son of man be (Matthew 24:27)," and John agreed, "Behold, he cometh with clouds; <u>and every eye shall see him, and they also which pierced him: and all kindreds of the earth shall wail because of him</u> (Revelation 1:7)."

According to St. Paul, Christ CANNOT come until two other events happen first, "Let no man deceive you by any means: for that day shall not come, <u>except there come a falling away first</u> - Apostasy of the Church, and <u>that man of sin be revealed, the son of perdition</u> – the Antichrist (2 Thessalonians 2:3)."

Christ's Coming, the resurrection, and the gathering of His Church will occur in a very orderly precise manner and not be an unpredictable haphazard secret, "Immediately <u>AFTER the tribulation of those days</u> shall the sun be darkened, and the moon shall not give her light, and the stars shall fall from heaven, and the powers of the heavens shall be shaken: 30 <u>AND THEN shall appear the sign of the Son of man in heaven</u>: <u>AND THEN shall all the tribes of the earth mourn, and they shall see the Son of man coming in the clouds of heaven with power and great glory</u>. 31And he shall send his angels with a great sound of a trumpet (the 'last trump' of the resurrection in 1 Corinthians 15:52), and they shall gather together his elect from the four winds (of earth), from one end of HEAVEN to the other (Matthew 24:29-31)."

St. Paul also gave various clues that mark the resurrection. The "mystery" and the "trumpet" are mentioned here, "Behold, I shew you <u>a mystery</u> (the mystery of the resurrection in Revelation 10:7); We shall not all sleep, but we shall all be changed, 52In a moment, in the twinkling of an eye, <u>at the last trump</u> (Matthew 24:31, Revelation 10:7, Revelation 11:15): for <u>the trumpet shall sound</u>, and <u>the dead shall be raised incorruptible</u> (the witnesses of Revelation 11:11), and we shall be changed (1 Corinthians 15:51-52)."

Besides the "mystery" and the "trumpet," the apostle also provided two other indicators (the shout & the voice of the archangel) to locate the resurrection, "For the Lord himself shall descend from heaven <u>with a shout</u> ('Come up hither!' Revelation 11:12), with the <u>voice of the archangel</u> ('Time shall be no more!' Revelation 10:6), and with <u>the trump of God</u> (the 'last trump,' 1 Corinthians 15:52, Matthew 24:31, Revelation 10:7, Revelation 11:15): and the dead in Christ shall rise first (the resurrection of the witnesses, Revelation 11:11): 17Then we which are alive and remain shall be caught up together with them in the clouds, to meet the Lord in the air (the gathering of Christ's Church, Revelation 11:12): and so shall we ever be with the Lord. 18Wherefore comfort one another with these words (1 Thessalonians 4:16-18)."

Following the resurrection, the Revelation portrays a glorious feast prepared for Christ's Church, "And I heard as it were the voice of a great multitude, and as the voice of many waters, and as the voice of mighty thunderings, saying, Alleluia: for the Lord God omnipotent reigneth. 7Let us be glad and rejoice, and give honour to him: <u>for the marriage of the Lamb is come, and his wife hath made herself ready</u>. 8And to her was granted that she should be arrayed in fine linen, clean and white: for the fine linen is the righteousness of saints. 9And he saith unto me, Write, <u>Blessed are they which are called unto the marriage supper of the Lamb</u>. And he saith unto me, These are the true sayings of God (Revelation 19:6-9)"

Hours before the Crucifixion, Jesus alluded to this same great feast while sharing the Sacrament with His disciples at the Last Supper, "And as they were eating, Jesus took bread, and blessed it, and brake it, and gave it to the disciples, and said, Take, eat; this is my body. 27And he took the cup, and gave thanks, and gave it to them, saying, Drink ye all of it; 28For this is my blood of the new testament, which is shed for many for the remission of sins. 29But I say unto you, <u>I will not drink henceforth of this fruit of the vine, until that day when I drink it new with you in my Father's kingdom</u> (Matthew 26:26-29)."

Isaiah added a profound detail for the purpose of this future meal, "And in this mountain shall the LORD of hosts make unto all people a feast of fat things, a feast of wines on the lees, of fat things full of marrow, of wines on the lees well refined. <u>7And he will destroy in this mountain the face of the covering cast over all people, and the veil that is spread over all nations. 8He will swallow up death in victory; and the Lord GOD will wipe away tears from off all faces; and the rebuke of his people shall he take away from off all the earth: for the LORD hath spoken it</u>. 9And it shall be said in that day, Lo, this is our God; we have waited for him, and he will save us: this is the LORD; we have waited for him, we will be glad and rejoice in his salvation (Isaiah 25:6-9)." Did you notice in verses 7-8 that God promised to remove the grave shroud from all nations while literally eating death for our sake during the magnificent feast He will prepare?

And so ends the resurrection as we head for Final Judgment!

CHAPTER FIVE

THE CONSUMMATION

Before going on, let us quickly review.

This is where our discussion started, "...it is appointed unto men once to die, but <u>after this</u> the judgment (Hebrews 9:27)."

"After this" ...the wildcard is time, our time, universal time, or God's eternal realm. How soon after death does judgment come? Is judgment immediate... or does it occur at the end of the Cosmos when God will create a New Heaven and Earth, or at some point in His eternity? Although the verse in Hebrews doesn't say, yet we have suggested that judgment accompanies resurrection... either the First Resurrection or the Last Resurrection. Thus, Karma happens when people's previous existence determines the events of their new life.

Next, we considered Jesus' words to the thief at the very moment of death, "Verily I say unto thee, Today shalt thou be with me in paradise (Luke 23:43)."

"IF" judgment is not immediate, then there must be a holding area until that evaluation eventually happens. For the Jews, that place of the dead was called Sheol. The Greeks named it Hades. The Early Church identified the residence of the departed as Paradise, which closely matches the Old Testament idea of being "gathered to the fathers," as in Psalms 49:19, Gen. 35:29, Gen. 47:30, Gen. 49:29 & 33, Num. 20:24 & 26, Num. 27:13, Num. 31:2, Deut.32:50, Judges 2:10, 2 Kings 22:50, Gen. 25:8 & 17.

Since the original "Garden of God" was where mankind began in the company of attending angels (Ezekiel 28:13) before both were eventually expelled to this natural world, what better location to be "gathered to the fathers" than Eden? Undoubtedly, Paradise will seem more like home than anywhere we have ever lived. Since the future is inscrutable, the past is the only concrete frame of reference we have. By the Early Church Father's account, Paradise was humanity's original state before being banished and thus, the gathering place for our ancestors after shedding their frail bodies. As a result, reentering Eden will feel like going home to rediscover the part of ourselves that was always missing… a much better association than we have known here and the underlying reason near-death subjects rarely want to resume their mortal existence.

For a moment I would like to digress by mentioning a question that readers will certainly ask at some point in the book, "Is Paradise and Sheol/Hades the only two destinations for souls immediately after death, or can the departed also remain close to the living here on earth?"

Though this survey of "Death and Beyond" is not intended to be a book about the paranormal, yet I must faithfully adhere to Scripture. Consequently, my faltering answer is, "Yes, for whatever reason, I think disembodied spirits can affiliate with this natural world without automatically resorting to either Paradise or Sheol/Hades!"

Why?

Please look carefully at this verse, "<u>And the sea gave up the dead which were in it</u>; and <u>death and hell delivered up the dead which were in them</u>: and they were judged every man according to their works (Revelation 20:13)."

We have already mentioned that "death and hell" will surrender their dead to be judged before the Great White Throne; however, did you notice that the sea will also relinquish those who died in its watery depths. Apparently, souls can attach themselves to places on earth that have absolutely nothing to do with the realm of the dead in the Third Heaven. The Bible does not explain why some of the deceased remained in or around the sea where they died. Thus, we can only speculate that their connection to the location was due to trauma, remorse, unfinished business, endearment to the living, or other reasons known only to them. Who knows? But Revelation 20:13 clearly confirms that some of the dead linger where they died.

I'm sure everyone (including myself) can share stories of personal experiences about someone who passed, but the time has come to return to Paradise…

Unlike many Church traditions that have flourished since the Reformation, early Christians accepted Jesus' words literally... Paradise was/is the original home intended for mankind until the "First Adam" was banished due to sin! However, Jesus Christ – the "Last Adam" restored humanity to Paradise when He preached for three days (after the Crucifixion until His Resurrection) to the disobedient dead who were locked in Hell/Sheol, "So also is the resurrection of the dead. It is sown in corruption; it is raised in incorruption: 43It is sown in dishonour; it is raised in glory: it is sown in weakness; it is raised in power: 44It is sown a natural body; it is raised a spiritual body. There is a natural body, and there is a spiritual body. 45And so it is written, The <u>first man Adam</u> was made a living soul (being); <u>the last Adam</u> was made a quickening (life-giving) spirit (1 Corinthians 15:45)." Thus, after the death of the carnal body, "Adam's children" are re-gathered in Paradise until the final judgment which is the culmination of all things.

Whether talking about Paradise or Sheol/Hell, we see both in the parable of Lazarus (Luke 16:19-31) with a happy place for the good and a not-so-happy place for the bad (which are visible to each other in the same heavenly dimension but divided by a vast space that prevents migration, except for those freed by Calvary). Paradise and/or Sheol/Hell both parallel the ancient doctrine of Purgatory, a limbo location between our natural lifetime and God's Eternity that spans universal time until the Final Judgment.

If Sheol/Hades was totally emptied after the Crucifixion (Eph. 4:8, 1 Pet. 3:19), then some believe that the dead are now with God the Father, but there is absolutely no Scripture that confirms that idea until the time of the resurrection when the Church comes out of Tribulation – Revelation 7:14 (except possibly for the dead martyrs under the Holy Altar next to the Heavenly Throne - Rev. 6:9). Consequently, the only other place for Hell's captives to go would be Paradise, right next door in the Third Heaven (2 Enoch 8-10, 2 Corinthians 12:2-4), albeit a distance away.

Yes, to be absent from the body is to be present with the Lord (2 Cor. 5:8), just as Jesus said He would join the thief in Paradise [Abraham's Bosom - the place of rest for both Lazarus (Luke 16:22) and the Prophet Samuel (1 Samuel 28:15)].

Being gathered to the fathers or being brought into Paradise matches most near-death experiences along with similar teachings from other civilizations. Every single culture on earth has believed in a "place of rest" after death; the Jews - Sheol, the Greeks - Elysium/Hades, Old Frisian - Helle, Old Norse - Hel, Germanic - Hölle, Gothic – Halja, Egyptian – Duat, Aztec – Mictlan, Mesopotamia – Irkalla, Old Welsh – Annwn, Old Irish – Mag Mell, American Hopi – Maski, Japanese – Yomi, Indonesian – Alam Ghaib, Philippine – Kasanaan, American Pueblo – Shipap, Slavic – Nav, Mongolian – Tamag, and on and on and on.

However, the Modern English "Hell" must not be confused with the Biblical doctrine of Final Damnation since both "Death and Hell (Hades/Sheol)" will be cast later into the Lake of Fire when our current universe is destroyed ahead of God's New Heaven and New Earth (Revelation 20:11 & 14). Consequently, the Greek Hades (the English Hell) is distinct from the place of Final Damnation known as the Lake of Fire (which comes later in order to receive the former).

Why should this matter? Well, the distinction between Sheol/Hades/Hell and the Lake of Fire underscores the horror of finally being separated from God's love... in Christ Jesus. Listen to what St. Paul asked, "Who shall separate us from the love of Christ? shall tribulation, or distress, or persecution, or famine, or nakedness, or peril, or sword (Romans 8:35)?"

This is a vital question, "Who can separate us from God's love?"

St. Paul proceeded to answer this way, "Nay, in all these things we are more than conquerors through him that loved us. 38For I am persuaded, that neither death, nor life, nor angels, nor principalities, nor powers, nor things present, nor things to come, 39Nor height, nor depth, nor any other creature, shall be able to separate us from the love of God, which is in Christ Jesus our Lord (Romans 8:37-39)."

Thus, no part of our present reality can separate us from God's love "which is in Christ Jesus" except for our own rejection of that same love! Rejecting Christ automatically disqualifies us from God's love since "God so loved the world, that he gave his only begotten Son, that whosoever believeth in him should not perish, but have everlasting life. 17For God sent not his Son into the world to condemn the world; but that the world through him might be saved (John 3:16-17)."

So, to escape judgment through God's love, we must believe in Jesus, "He that believeth on him is not condemned: but he that believeth not is condemned already, because he hath not believed in the name of the only begotten Son of God. 19And this is the condemnation, that light is come into the world, and men loved darkness rather than light, because their deeds were evil (John 3:18-19)."

Here rests the horror of Final Damnation since Judgment is still pending. Functioning as a holding place for the departed during Cosmic Time prior to Eternity, Paradise is not permanent in any way! God emptied Paradise once when our father Adam disobeyed, and the Almighty can do it again when the situation demands. In the future, there will be a reason to eliminate Paradise.

Undoubtedly, Paradise will be vacated and shut down during the First Resurrection, when Christ sends the angels with the sound of the last trumpet to gather His Church from Heaven (Matthew 24:31). According to St. Paul's near-death experience, this gathering will be made in the Third Heaven (2 Corinthians 12:2). Later, Hell/Sheol will also be emptied and cast into the Lake of Fire at the Great White Throne Judgment when Universal Time ends before the next creation cycle on the eve of a new reality (Revelation

20:13-15). In 2 Enoch, we learned that Hell/Sheol was also in the Third Heaven. By the time God is ready to create again, much of Heaven will be abandoned after drastically shaking up the old order.

Foreshadowing the end of all things, St. Paul shared an ominous warning, "See that ye refuse not him that speaketh. For if they escaped not who refused him that spake on earth, much more shall not we escape, if we turn away from him that speaketh from heaven: 26Whose voice then shook the earth: but now he hath promised, saying, <u>Yet once more I shake not the earth only, but also heaven. 27And this word, Yet once more, signifieth the removing of those things that are shaken, as of things that are made, that those things which cannot be shaken may remain</u>. 28Wherefore we receiving a kingdom which cannot be moved, let us have grace, whereby we may serve God acceptably with reverence and godly fear: 29<u>For our God is a consuming fire</u> (Hebrews 12:25-29)."

"And this word, Yet once more, signifieth the removing of those things that are shaken, as of <u>THINGS THAT ARE MADE</u>," and except for the infinite Godhead, everything that we can imagine… was made, including Heaven and the angels. When God speaks of the Consummation and says, "I'm shaking EVERYTHING in Heaven and Earth to remove anything that can be destroyed in order to save what remains," then we should fathom the utter and absolute cataclysm that faces us! In the end, the only things spared will be saved by God's Grace alone, "For by grace are ye saved through faith; and that not of yourselves: it is the gift of God (Ephesians 2:8)!"

Changes are coming in the future from the top down, as suggested by St. Peter, "For the time is come that judgment must begin at the house of God: and if it first begin at us, what shall the end be of them that obey not the gospel of God (1 Peter 4:17)?"

But what will the Consummation look like?

The Old Testament prophets were already discussing the final catastrophe long before Christ ever appeared.

"The sun shall be turned into darkness, and the moon into blood, before the great and the terrible day of the LORD come (Joel 2:31)," and "The sun and the moon shall be darkened, and the stars shall withdraw their shining (Joel 3:15)."

"And all the host of heaven shall be dissolved, and the heavens shall be rolled together as a scroll: and all their host shall fall down, as the leaf falleth off from the vine, and as a falling fig from the fig tree (Isaiah 34:4)."

Eventually, Jesus foreshadowed the same awesome event in the Gospels.

"Immediately after the tribulation of those days shall the sun be darkened, and the moon shall not give her light, and the stars shall fall from heaven, <u>and the powers of the heavens shall be shaken</u> (Matthew 24:29)," and "In those days, after that tribulation, the sun shall be darkened, and the moon shall not give her light, 25And the stars of heaven shall fall, <u>and the powers that are in heaven shall be shaken</u> (Mark 13:24-25)."

Later, John chronicled the cataclysm this way, "...The sun became black as sackcloth of hair, and the moon became as blood; 13And the stars of heaven fell unto the earth, even as a fig tree casteth her untimely figs, when she is shaken of a mighty wind (Revelation 6:13)."

At the same time, notice St. Peter's description of the destruction of the realms of Heaven and the obliteration of Earth on the eve of the New Creation, "But, beloved, be not ignorant of this one thing, <u>that one day is with the Lord as a thousand years, and a thousand years as one day</u> (Once again, we notice the relative nature of time). 9The Lord is not slack concerning his promise, as some men count slackness; but is longsuffering to us-ward, not willing that any should perish, but that all should come to repentance. 10But the day of the Lord will come as a thief in the night; in the which the <u>heavens</u> (plural – the multiple levels of Heaven not merely the natural sky) shall pass away with a great noise, <u>and the elements shall melt with fervent heat, the earth also and the works that are therein shall be burned up</u>. 11Seeing then that <u>ALL THESE THINGS</u> shall be <u>dissolved</u> (Greek – lyō, to loosen or break apart into elemental/sub-atomic parts), what manner of persons ought ye to be in all holy conversation and godliness, 12Looking for and hasting unto the coming of the day of God, wherein the HEAVENS BEING ON FIRE shall be <u>dissolved</u>, and the <u>elements shall melt with fervent heat</u>? 13Nevertheless we, according to his promise, look for <u>NEW HEAVENS</u> and a <u>NEW EARTH</u>, wherein dwelleth righteousness (2 Peter 3:8-13)."

So, where do you plan to be when God Almighty sets His Heavens on fire and dissolves the Earth into sub-atomic particles to begin again? I hope after you've died, your life is hid with Christ in God and written in the volume of THE BOOK in order to be part of His plan for the New Creation that's coming (Colossians 3:3, Hebrews 10:7).

Like anyone else, physicists try to understand the future by knowing what existed prior to the moment of Creation - the "BIG BANG" in the scientific vernacular of quantum mechanics.

Undoubtedly, the answer is, "An older reality than the one we know."

Imagine one among a myriad of seeded points in deep space, cloaked inside an inscrutable void where "He made darkness his secret place (Psalms 18:11)," that a threshold was crossed, a critical mass was reached, a thought was born, and a word was spoken. Instantly, a spark flickered, and from that primeval glimmer... an unfathomable effulgence of energy exploded throughout the former cosmos, sanitizing the farthest reaches of the old universe that was subsequently swept out of the way, "Through faith we understand that the worlds were framed by the word of God, so that things which are seen were not made of things which do appear (Hebrews 11:3)." Like successive troughs and waves generated on the surface of a lake hit by a stone, Almighty God began creating again!

And the word was this… "In the beginning God created the heaven and the earth. And the earth was without form, and void; and darkness was upon the face of the deep. And the Spirit of God moved upon the face of the waters. And God said, Let there be light: and there was light… Of old hast thou laid the foundation of the earth: and the heavens are the work of thy hands. They shall perish, but thou shalt endure: yea, all of them shall wax old like a garment; as a vesture shalt thou change them, and they shall be changed… Lift up your eyes to the heavens, and look upon the earth beneath: for the heavens shall vanish away like smoke, and the earth shall wax old like a garment, and they that dwell therein shall die in like manner… For the former troubles will be forgotten and hidden from My sight. For behold, I will create new heavens and a new earth. The former things will not be remembered, nor will they come to mind… And I saw a great white throne, and him that sat on it, from whose face the earth and the heaven fled away; and there was found no place for them… And I saw a new heaven and a new earth: for the first heaven and the first earth were passed away… (Genesis 1:1-3, Psalms 102:25-26, Isaiah 51:6, Isaiah 65:16-17, Revelation 20:11, Revelation 21:21)."

Briefly, we should consider the phrase "the first heaven and the first earth" mentioned in Revelation 21:21 and realize that two possibilities exist.

One... this present reality is literally part of the first and only Cosmos that God ever created, but if true, then we are left with the problem of explaining the angels' appearance without any record of their origin from Genesis to Revelation. Not eternally existent with God, they had to be created but where and when - Ezekiel 28:13-14?

Two... Since "the former troubles will be forgotten and hidden (Isaiah 65:16)," and "the former things will not be remembered, nor will they come to mind (Isaiah 65:17)," then this present Cosmos figuratively exists as the "the first heaven and the first earth" without any recollection of the one that came before it.

You decide, but meanwhile, the Church plausibly has a vital role to fill before the Consummation regarding the dead.

CHAPTER SIX

BUT UNTIL THEN... MEDIATION FOR THE DEAD

As we said before, the prophet Isaiah foreshadowed the messianic ministry of Jesus Christ, "The Spirit of the Lord GOD is upon me; because the LORD hath anointed me to preach good tidings unto the meek; he hath sent me to bind up the brokenhearted, <u>to proclaim liberty to the captives, and the opening of the prison to them that are bound</u> (Isaiah 61:1)."

In Ephesians 4:7-10, St. Paul alluded to how Jesus fulfilled His prophetic mission of "proclaiming liberty to the captives, and the opening of the prison to them that are bound" while interceding for the dead after the crucifixion, "But unto <u>every one of us is given grace according to the measure of the gift of Christ</u>. 8Wherefore he saith, <u>When he ascended up on high, he led captivity captive, and gave gifts unto men. 9Now that he ascended, what is it but that he also descended first into the lower parts of the earth? 10He that descended is the same also that ascended up far above all heavens,</u> that he might fill all things"

Notice, the apostle said that "everyone of us" was offered grace "according to the measure of the gift of Christ," even in the "lower parts of the earth." Without quibbling whether the location was the "third heaven" or the "lower parts of the earth," St. Peter clearly identified the recipients of the Gospel message which continued three days from the Crucifixion to the Resurrection, "For Christ also hath once suffered for sins, the just for the unjust, that he might bring us to God, being put to death in the flesh, but quickened by the Spirit: 19By which also <u>he went and preached unto the spirits in prison; 20Which sometime were disobedient, when once the longsuffering of God waited in the days of Noah, while the ark was a preparing, wherein few, that is, eight souls were saved by water</u> (1 Peter 3:18-20)."

Indisputably, Jesus' prison ministry of Isaiah 61extended all the way to Sheol/Hell when He preached to the "<u>spirits in prison which sometime were disobedient</u>, when once the longsuffering of God waited in the days of Noah, while the ark was a preparing." Thus, we know who received Christ's message of Grace, we know where they were when they received it, and we even know when they died before finally receiving God's promise!

Consequently, we can understand the divine commission that Jesus spoke to Peter regarding the supreme authority of Christ's Church, "He saith unto them, But whom say ye that I am? 16 And Simon Peter answered and said, Thou art the Christ, the Son of the living God. 17 And Jesus answered and said unto him, Blessed art thou, Simon Barjona: for flesh and blood hath not revealed it unto thee, but my Father which is in heaven. 18 And I say also unto thee, That thou art Peter, and upon this rock (Jesus is the Christ) I will build my church; <u>and the gates of hell shall not prevail against it</u> (Matthew 16:15-18)." Please understand that the statement, "the gates of hell shall not prevail against it" has absolutely nothing to do with Hell/Sheol/Hades attacking the Church, but rather the Church bursting through the gates of Hell/Sheol/Hades to gain entry.

Established on Peter's true confession, "Thou art the Christ, the Son of the living God," Jesus promised to build a Church that would have the ultimate authority to successfully invade Hell/Sheol – the realm of the dead whose prison would not be able to withstand an attack. But why would Christ want His Church to pass beyond the gates of the grave to access the dead?

Jesus continued speaking to Peter, "And I will give unto thee the keys of the kingdom of heaven: and whatsoever thou shalt bind on earth shall be bound in heaven: and whatsoever thou shalt loose on earth shall be loosed in heaven (Matthew 16: 19)." The very same promise is repeated in Matthew 18:18, "Verily I say unto you, Whatsoever ye shall bind on earth shall be bound in heaven: and whatsoever ye shall loose on earth shall be loosed in heaven."

What is significant about the Church being endorsed by Heaven to "bind things on earth" or to "loose things on earth?" What is the application or benefit of such spiritual strength? Consider what Jesus said in John 20:23,

"Whosesoever sins ye remit (forgive), they are remitted (forgiven) unto them; and whosesoever sins ye retain, they are retained."

While many Christians in the West have carelessly neglected the kingdom authority that they receive through Jesus Christ's Resurrection, the Church literally has the power to intercede for sin by baptism all the way to the domain of the dead. Let's finish St. Peter's statement about Jesus preaching to the spirits in prison which sometime were disobedient, "The like figure whereunto even baptism doth also now save us (not the putting away of the filth of the flesh, but the answer of a good conscience toward God,) by the resurrection of Jesus Christ: 22 Who is gone into heaven, and is on the right hand of God; angels and authorities and powers being made subject unto him (1 Peter 3:21-22)."

Someone will argue, "Well, that was appropriate for Christ, but Christians don't share that same ministry!"

However, listen to Jesus' words in John 14:12, "Verily, verily, I say unto you, He that believeth on me, the works that I do shall he do also; and greater works than these shall he do; because I go unto my Father," and "If thou canst believe, all things are possible to him that believeth (Mark 9:23)." If we literally accept Christ's statement, then the Church has greater authority in matching His ministry, not less… even when attacking the gates of Hell/Hades/Sheol.

For this purpose, St. Paul was very specific regarding intercession/mediation for the dead, "For he hath put all things under his feet. But when he saith all things are put under him, it is manifest that he is excepted, which did put all things under him. 28 And when all things shall be subdued unto him, then shall the Son also himself be subject unto him that put all things under him, that God may be all in all. 29 <u>Else what shall they do which are baptized for the dead, if the dead rise not at all? why are they then baptized for the dead</u> (1 Corinthians 15:27-29)?"

After carefully noting that everything in Creation is placed under Christ's authority (except for God Almighty who singlehandedly elevated His Son to that lofty position) the apostle addressed the justification of being vicariously "baptized for the dead due to the Resurrection." Once again, we witness Jesus' three-day ministry in Hell/Hades/Sheol following the Crucifixion. The miracle of our Lord's Resurrection gives us the authority and power to mediate/intercede for the dead just as Jesus did while His body rested in the grave. <u>Obviously, the intercessor who is baptized in proxy for the dead, should already be a Christian and baptized into Christ themselves before trying to represent someone in death since Christ specifically gave the "Keys of Divine Authority" to His Church and not the world, "For as many of you as have been baptized into Christ have put on Christ (Galatians 3:27).</u>"

Although mediating for the dead is an unusual practice in the West, both the Jews and the Early Church shared the tradition of making intercessory prayers for the departed.

Following the death of a loved one, the Jews pray one year for the soul. The prayer is called the "Kaddish." Jews believe that righteous individuals go through a period of refinement following death in which they may amend for past mistakes. The living can assist them during this period of refinement by interceding to God in their behalf. The Catholic Church has the same tradition of a place called Purgatory, and while the dead amend for past mistakes, the living help them by intercessory prayer.

Scripture clearly attests that God respects the role/function of an intercessor best portrayed by Moses, "Yet now, if thou wilt forgive their sin… and if not, blot me, I pray thee, out of thy book which thou hast written (Exodus 32:32)," and "Moses said unto Aaron, Take a censer, and put fire therein from off the altar, and put on incense, and go quickly unto the congregation, and make an atonement for them: for there is wrath gone out from the LORD; the plague is begun (Numbers 16:46)."

Also in Ezekiel 22:30-31, we read, "And I sought for a man among them, that should make up the hedge, and stand in the gap before me for the land, that I should not destroy it: but I found none. 31 Therefore have I poured out mine indignation upon them; I have consumed them with the fire of my wrath: their own way have I recompensed upon their heads, saith the Lord GOD."

Sadly, Hell/Hades/Sheol is filled with people who are neglected by Christ's Church because of a frail misapplied argument that nothing can be done beyond this life to amend for sin, "If the clouds be full of rain, they empty themselves upon the earth: and if the tree fall toward the south, or toward the north, in the place where the tree falleth, there it shall be (Ecclesiastes 11:3);" however, Solomon was not referring to either the dead locked in Sheol or the ministry of intercession for them. Furthermore, denying mediation for the dead by saying "a tree rests in the same direction it falls," ignores the action of a logger who hooks a chain to the trunk and drags it wherever he will... which is an allegory for the ministry of Christ's Church. By the power of His Cross and the Empty Tomb, Jesus said that we could invade Hell/Hades/Sheol and set the captives free.

The crux of the question simply rests on the issue of whether God's Grace reaches beyond life to the grave. Consider Jesus' words, "And whosoever speaketh a word against the Son of man, it shall be forgiven him: but whosoever speaketh against the Holy Ghost, it shall not be forgiven him, neither in this world, neither in the world to come (Matthew 12:32)."

In the above passage, Jesus is qualifying sins that can and cannot be forgiven. Please notice that all sins can be forgiven but one. Except for blasphemy against the Holy Spirit which can NEVER be forgiven, God's Grace has the potential of being applied "in this world and in the world to come" extending beyond death.

Tragically, the debate in Western Christianity over

mediation for the dead stems from a crime committed against God's Word during the Reformation. Although I am a proud Protestant, yet a Catholic priest named Martin Luther gutted long-established doctrine over the issue of revenue that the Church incurred from prayers for the dead.

Three hundred years before the birth of Christ, the fourteen books of the Apocrypha were part of the Old Testament Canon when the Hebrew Scripture was translated into the Greek Septuagint (325–350 BC) - the Bible of Jesus, St. Peter, and St. Paul. Later, at the Church Council of Laodicea (364 AD), Hippo (393 AD), and Carthage (397 AD), the Canon – our Bible was officially sealed to prevent new books from being added or old books from being removed. Fifteen hundred years following the birth of Jesus, the very same books continued to be part of our Bible after the Greek Scripture was translated into Latin by St. Jerome in 382 AD. However, five hundred years ago during the Reformation, Luther was offended by several books that weakened his position against the Pope. So, just as King Jehudi used his little penknife on Jeremiah's scroll (Jeremiah 36:23), the noted reformer gutted the Old Testament Canon to his liking, despite eighteen hundred years of biblical integrity. He also tried to remove Hebrews, James, Jude, and the Revelation from the New Testament. However, there was too much public opposition, so he relocated the contested books to the very back of the Bible to show his disapproval.

In the twelfth chapter of 2 Maccabees - a book vital for studying Daniel but one that Luther removed, there is ample proof for offerings made to pray for the dead in hopes of a righteous resurrection, "On the next day, as by that time it had become necessary, Judas and his men went to take up the bodies of the fallen and to bring them back to lie with their kinsmen in the sepulchres of their fathers. 40 Then under the tunic of every one of the dead they found sacred tokens of the idols of Jam'nia, which the law forbids the Jews to wear. And it became clear to all that this was why these men had fallen. 41 So they all blessed the ways of the Lord, the righteous Judge, who reveals the things that are hidden; 42 and they turned to prayer, beseeching that the sin which had been committed might be wholly blotted out. And the noble Judas exhorted the people to keep themselves free from sin, for they had seen with their own eyes what had happened because of the sin of those who had fallen. 43 He also took up a collection, man by man, to the amount of two thousand drachmas of silver, and sent it to Jerusalem to provide for a sin offering. In doing this he acted very well and honorably, taking account of the resurrection. 44 For if he were not expecting that those who had fallen would rise again, it would have been superfluous and foolish to pray for the dead. 45 But if he was looking to the splendid reward that is laid up for those who fall asleep in godliness, it was a holy and pious thought. Therefore he made atonement

<u>for the dead, that they might be delivered from their sin</u> (2 Maccabees 12:39-45)."

Thus, the universal Church once mediated for the departed because of the primal Jewish custom of offering the Kaddish – the prayer for the dead. Consequently, Luther had absolutely NO RIGHT to tamper with established Scripture or to change ancient doctrine while waging war on the Pope.

Having addressed the topic of intercessory prayer and baptism for the dead, what type of baptism is proper to be used… immersion, pouring, or sprinkling? Once again, this divisive question has polarized the Church.

Surprisingly, those who exclusively promote immersion have absolutely no Scripture to do so, apart from a metaphor on burial that St. Paul stated, "<u>Therefore we are buried with him by baptism into death</u>: that like as Christ was raised up from the dead by the glory of the Father, even so we also should walk in newness of life (Romans 6:4)," and "<u>Buried with him in baptism</u>, wherein also ye are risen with him through the faith of the operation of God, who hath raised him from the dead (Colossians 2:12)." But at no time does the Bible say, "Submerse only!"

To the contrary, Scripture actually endorses sprinkling as a form of baptism for conversion from sin, "<u>Then will I sprinkle clean water upon you, and ye shall be clean</u>: from all your filthiness, and from all your idols, will I cleanse you. <u>26A new heart also will I give you, and a new spirit will I</u>

put within you: and I will take away the stony heart out of your flesh, and I will give you an heart of flesh. 27And I will put my spirit within you, and cause you to walk in my statutes, and ye shall keep my judgments, and do them (Ezekiel 36:25:27)." However, by no means should this verse be used to exclude immersion.

Probably the most equitable doctrine for baptism comes from a primitive Christian document that several Early Church Fathers wanted added to the official Canon, but was excluded. This writing was called the Didache - "The Teaching of the Lord to the Gentiles by the Twelve Apostles." The Didache was the earliest recorded catechism of the Church that listed the vital tenets of Christian faith. While 18th-century historians claimed the Didache appeared in the second century, today most scholars agree that the document was compiled in the first century, as early as 49-50 AD under James the Just near the time of the Pauline Epistles and possibly even while Christ was still ministering. If this is the case, then the Didache might be the earliest piece of Jewish-Christian literature the Church has, predating both the letters of St. Paul and the Gospels.

Although quite concise with only 2,300 words, the Didache covers everything, as any good catechism should. At the beginning, the Didache addresses moral behavior with a section in chapters 1–6 called "The Two Ways, the Way of Life and the Way of Death." Next come the orders for baptism, fasting, and Sacrament in chapters 7–10. The third part deals with the ministry and the care of apostles, prophets, bishops, and deacons who are encouraged to support themselves and not overburden the Church (chapters 11–15). Chapter 16 concludes with a prophecy about the Antichrist and Jesus' Second Coming.

Since the early Jewish sect of Christianity began in a desert climate, the Didache recommends three forms of baptism depending on the presence of water, "And concerning baptism, baptize this way: Having first said all these things, baptize into the name of the Father, and of the Son, and of the Holy Spirit, in living water. But if you have no living water, baptize into other water; and if you cannot do so in cold water, do so in warm. But if you have neither, pour out water three times upon the head into the name of Father and Son and Holy Spirit. But before the baptism let the baptizer fast, and the baptized, and whoever else can; but you shall order the baptized to fast one or two days before (Chapter 7- Concerning Baptism)." This is a little something that I like to call... common sense!

The sacrament of baptism was simply performed in a desert climate by the most logical method available. If there was enough water, then they immersed. If there was not enough water, then they took what little water they had to either pour or sprinkle (Ezekiel 36:25:27). But the modern Western church has created its own pharisaical traditions... just as Jesus' contemporaries did. On a personal note, I once offered to baptize (by sprinkling) a young man who accepted Jesus while dying in a hospital bed of terminal cancer. Instantly the fellow's mother balked at the idea by saying, "We don't do it that way!"

I took the lady out in the hall and asked, "Your son has accepted Jesus as his savior. So, are you going to forbid him baptism before he leaves this life based on a technicality?"

After thinking a moment, she sobbed, "No, please baptize him!"

And we did! The mother quickly gathered up some hospital towels to place above his head and next to his face while a friend of the family got a small paper cup of water, and in the name of "God the Father, Jesus Christ His Son, and the Holy Spirit" I baptized the boy ten minutes before he lapsed into a coma.

The Didache's order of baptism is also confirmed by archaeological evidence. Nearly all first century Christian mosaics depict baptism by either pouring or sprinkling. So, where exactly did we get this unbending entrenched attitude that "if it's not immersion... then it counts for nothing?" Obviously, the idea was just another construct of human nature apart from God's Word that added to the fragmentation of Christ's Church.

While concluding, I am personally compelled to state a disclaimer. Our discussion on mediation for the dead involves interceding to God through prayer and baptism for the sake of the dearly departed but adamantly does not include any effort to contact or communicate with those who have passed since that occult practice is expressly forbidden by Scripture, "Regard not them that have familiar spirits (mediums or psychics), neither seek after wizards (witchcraft), to be defiled by them: I am the LORD your God (Leviticus 19:31)."

"And the soul that turneth after such as have familiar spirits (mediums or psychics), and after wizards (witchcraft), to go a whoring after them, I will even set my face against that soul, and will cut him off from among his people (Leviticus 20:6)."

"There shall not be found among you any one that maketh his son or his daughter to pass through the fire (child sacrifice), or that useth divination (fortune-telling), or an observer of times (interpret omens), or an enchanter (sorcery), or a witch, 11Or a charmer (cast spells), or a consulter with familiar spirits (mediums or psychics), or a wizard (male witch), or a necromancer (call the spirits of the dead). 12For all that do these things are an abomination unto the LORD: and because of these abominations the LORD thy God doth drive them out from before thee. 13Thou shalt be perfect with the LORD thy God. 14For these nations, which thou shalt possess, hearkened unto observers of times, and unto diviners: but as for thee, the LORD thy God hath not suffered thee so to do (Deuteronomy 18:10-14)."

Why do we NOT communicate with the dead? There are sinister entities lurking in the shadows that have absolutely nothing to do with the souls of the dearly departed. These malevolent beings came into existence during the days of Noah and have roamed dark places ever since, constantly seeking mortal flesh to control. Trying to contact the dead is an open invitation to be attacked by these malignant spiritual forces. Thus, our conversation must exclusively be with God alone and no one else.

CHAPTER SEVEN

HERE WE GO AGAIN... A HINT OF REINCARNATION

The horrible "R" Word (reincarnation) is shunned by many in the Church despite one irrefutable instance of the phenomenon in the Bible and possibly even two. However, if these two examples are truly cases of reincarnation, still the doctrine is not promoted generally by Scripture. Instead, I merely accept that God can do anything He likes to accomplish His will... whether by life or by death.

We will begin our search for Scriptural Reincarnation by reading this verse, "Behold, I will send you Elijah the prophet before the coming of the great and dreadful day of the LORD (Malachi 4:5)." By the time Malachi wrote this prophecy, Elijah had been gone for hundreds of years.

Alluding to the Consummation, Malachi said that God would send Elijah back to earth again, "to turn the heart of the fathers to the children, and the heart of the children to their fathers (Malachi 4:6)," before God came to destroy the earth.

Similar to Enoch, the prophet Elijah did not die but was taken to Heaven by God, "...There appeared a chariot of fire, and horses of fire, and parted them (Elijah and

Elisha) both asunder; and Elijah went up by a whirlwind into heaven (2 Kings 2:11)." So, for Malachi's prophecy to be fulfilled, the Almighty would either send Elijah back to earth in the man's original Old Testament form or allow him to be reborn before the End of Time... which would be reincarnation.

Now, I can already hear the naysayers growling, "What Malachi really meant was..." but before we throw the baby out with the bath water, why not allow the story to reach its climax.

After John the Baptist was born to Elizabeth and Zechariah (Luke 1:7&40), he grew up to be the wild man from the Jordan (Matthew 3:4) who took Judea by storm (Matthew 11:7). Instantly, everyone wanted to hear the fellow speak as multitudes were baptized by the frontier preacher. Among the crowd, temple officials from Jerusalem came to discover what was occurring and to possibly avoid political blowback if the man's ministry created problems for the Roman occupiers. Without wasting time, the priests and Levites asked, "Who are you (John 1:19)?"

Immediately, the Baptist answered, "I'm not Christ (John 1:20)!"

However, the religious elite ignored who he was not, to learn who he was, "What then? Art thou Elias? And he saith, I am not. Art thou that prophet (John 1:21)?"

Consequently, the temple authority suspected that

Malachi's prophecy was being fulfilled, but John did not recognize himself as Elijah and answered, "No."

There was only one choice left. Surely John was the Prophet that God mentioned to Moses, "The LORD thy God will raise up unto thee a Prophet from the midst of thee, of thy brethren, <u>like unto me</u> (God); unto him ye shall hearken; 18I will raise them up a Prophet from among their brethren, <u>like unto thee</u> (Moses), and will put my words in his mouth; and he shall speak unto them all that I shall command him. 19And it shall come to pass, that whosoever will not hearken unto my words which he shall speak in my name, I will require it of him (Deuteronomy 18:15, 18-19)."

Unquestionably, this new Prophet would have a phenomenal ministry since He was to be "like God and like Moses," divine and human at the very same time, but John professed that he was not that Prophet either! So, who exactly was this Baptist?

Growing impatient, the Jerusalem committee demanded, "Who art thou? that we may give an answer to them that sent us. What sayest thou of thyself (John 1:22-23)?"

Typical of unassuming John, the Baptist answered that he was a faceless nobody, "I am the voice of one crying in the wilderness, Make straight the way of the Lord, as said the prophet Esaias (John 1:23)."

Disappointed that John was not the Christ, Elijah, or that Prophet, they criticized the man's lack of authority to make disciples through the rite of baptism (as Elijah had done along the Jordan with the "sons of the prophets" - 2 Kings 2:3), "Why baptizest thou then, if thou be not that Christ, nor Elias, neither that prophet (John 1:25)?"

The preacher proceeded to inform his interrogators that the Prophet who God promised Moses was in the crowd, although the Temple authority had not noticed, "I baptize with water: but there standeth one among you, whom ye know not; 27He it is, who coming after me is preferred before me, whose shoe's latchet I am not worthy to unloose (John 1:26-27)." They were so close to the truth but could not see!

Sadly, blindness is common to all, even John the Baptist who did not recognize himself as Elijah... although the Glorious Prophet did! On the eve of John's martyrdom, listen to what Jesus said about his faithful cousin, "Verily I say unto you, Among them that are born of women there hath not risen a greater than John the Baptist: notwithstanding he that is least in the kingdom of heaven is greater than he. 12And from the days of John the Baptist until now the kingdom of heaven suffereth violence, and the violent take it by force. 13For all the prophets and the law prophesied until John. 14And if ye will receive it, this is Elias, which was for to come. 15He that hath ears to hear, let him hear (Matthew 11:11-15)."

Even before revealing the earthshaking revelation, Jesus knew that some in the audience would not be able to receive (accept) that John the Baptist was really reincarnated Elijah, reborn as Elizabeth and Zechariah's son. Emphasizing the point, Christ admonished His listeners to open their ears and hear, but even today, people ignore Jesus' words by refusing the possibility of John's double identity, both as Elijah and the Baptist.

So, if John was the first indisputable case of reincarnation mentioned in our Bible, then who comes second? Well, we're already really close to the other example when talking about the Baptist. Number two would be his illustrious cousin... Jesus Christ! Does that surprise you? It shouldn't! All through the Old Testament, we notice subtle appearances of Jesus in His pre-incarnate, albeit physical form.

Probably the first time we notice God's Son is in Paradise with our father Adam, "And they heard the <u>voice</u> of the LORD God <u>walking</u> in the garden in the cool of the day (Genesis 3:8)." Besides having an audible voice, God took a physical body since He was "walking."

Possibly, we see Jesus the next time with Jacob, "And Jacob was left alone; <u>and there wrestled a man with him until the breaking of the day</u>. 25And when he saw that he prevailed not against him, he touched the hollow of his thigh; and the hollow of Jacob's thigh was out of joint, as he wrestled with him. 26And he said, Let me go, for the day breaketh. And he said, I will not let thee go, except thou bless me. 27And he said unto him, What is thy name? And he said, Jacob. 28And he said, <u>Thy name shall be called no more Jacob, but Israel: for as a prince hast thou power with</u>

God and with men, and hast prevailed (Jacob wrestled all nightlong with the physical God and won. Consequently, the man was renamed Israel - Prince). 29And Jacob asked him, and said, Tell me, I pray thee, thy name. And he said, Wherefore is it that thou dost ask after my name (After wrestling for hours with God, Jacob secretly knew his divine opponent and didn't need to ask)? And he (God) blessed him (Jacob/Israel) there. (Genesis 32:24-29)."

Some try to say that Jacob wrestled with an angel, but the Scripture clearly proves otherwise, "And Jacob called the name of the place Peniel: for I have seen God face to face, and my life is preserved (Genesis 32:30)." Again, Jacob's stranger was not a spiritual entity but rather a physical form of God who had a man's face... the pre-incarnate Christ with a flesh and bone body!

Later we see Jesus in Babylon with the captives from Judah, "And these three men, Shadrach, Meshach, and Abednego, fell down bound into the midst of the burning fiery furnace. 24Then Nebuchadnezzar the king was astonied, and rose up in haste, and spake, and said unto his counsellers, Did not we cast three men bound into the midst of the fire? They answered and said unto the king, True, O king. 25He answered and said, Lo, I see four men loose, walking in the midst of the fire, and they have no hurt; and the form of the fourth is like the Son of God (Daniel 3:23-)."

Without any room for debate, the stranger's identity was perfectly clear – the Son of God!

Probably the best description of Jesus' pre-incarnate manifestation is provided by St. Paul while teaching about Christ's superior priesthood, "For this Melchisedec, king of Salem, priest of the most high God, who met Abraham returning from the slaughter of the kings, and blessed him; 2To whom also Abraham gave a tenth part of all; first being by interpretation King of righteousness, and after that also King of Salem, which is, King of peace; 3Without father, without mother, without descent, having neither beginning of days, nor end of life; but made like unto the Son of God; abideth a priest continually. 4Now consider how great this man was, unto whom even the patriarch Abraham gave the tenth of the spoils...15And it is yet far more evident: for that after the similitude of Melchisedec there ariseth another priest (Jesus), 16Who is made, not after the law of a carnal commandment, but after the power of an endless life. 17For he testifieth, Thou art a priest for ever after the order of Melchisedec... (Jesus) 21The Lord sware and will not repent, Thou art a priest for ever after the order of Melchisedec (Jesus). 22By so much was Jesus made a surety of a better testament (Hebrews 7:1-4, 15-17, 21-22)."

Whether in Paradise with Adam or receiving an offering from Abraham or confronting Jacob at the ford Jabbok or defending the Hebrews in the fiery furnace or being born in a lowly stable or saving my wretched soul by dying on a cruel Cross, my Savior... Jesus Christ... God's Son has been there through it all, and if that's not reincarnation, then it's getting mighty close!

Granted, one indisputable case of reincarnation in the Bible... or possibly two, still does not make the anomaly the norm or a universal doctrine, but as I said before, Almighty God can do anything He chooses to accomplish His will... without getting my approval first. Thus, if John the Baptist was Elijah as Jesus said, then so be it.

In the end, we arrive at the beginning where we said in Chapter One that a conundrum springs from the relative nature of time, and there are three: Lifetime, Cosmic Time, and God's Time. The only parameters are marked by the moment of death and the beginning of judgment which identifies an interval between our Lifetime and the end of Cosmic Time, leaving only God's Time before He creates again. During the interlude between death, the resurrection, and judgment - Hebrews 9:27, anything can happen depending on God's will. Experiencing the eerie occurrence of déjà vu, I have often wondered if our consciousness might loop back on itself at the moment of future death to intersect with previous experience so our youth detects an older version of awareness. So, did you get that? Nonetheless, without a Scriptural basis, my conjecture has no more merit than saying the anomaly is merely a chemical condition of the brain. We must save that discussion for another book!

If our exploration of "Death and Beyond" has seemed

circular in nature, then it matches one of my favorite passages from Solomon's book of Ecclesiastes, "One generation passeth away, and another generation cometh... 5The sun also ariseth, and the sun goeth down, and hasteth to his place where he arose. 6The wind goeth toward the south, and turneth about unto the north; it whirleth about continually, and the wind returneth again according to his circuits. 7All the rivers run into the sea; yet the sea is not full; unto the place from whence the rivers come, thither they return again... 9The thing that hath been, it is that which shall be; and that which is done is that which shall be done: and there is no new thing under the sun. 10Is there anything whereof it may be said, See, this is new? it hath been already of old time, which was before us. 11There is no remembrance of former things; neither shall there be any remembrance of things that are to come with those that shall come after (Ecclesiastes 1:4-11)."

As we conclude our scriptural investigation, one last question should be asked, "If predestined believers were recorded in the Book of Life before this Cosmos began, and if they are to be included in the creation of a new Heaven and Earth by having their names written in that Book of Life, then will the Elect appear during the next iteration in their present bodies?"

Initially, we might say, "Yes, this is the body that we keep!" However, what about precious individuals who suffer from severe deformities, disabilities, and handicaps? Will these souls transition into the same body or get a new one on the other side? If the Chosen who appear in the Book of Life preceded this Creation and travel through the present reality into the next Cosmic Cycle, then it seems logical to think that their enduring spiritual entity will be clothed with a brand-new body that might look different from the one they now have, and that my friend is the essence of reincarnation. The important thing to remember is this… regardless of our outer shell, John promised, "Beloved, now are we the sons of God, and it doth not yet appear what we shall be: but we know that, when he shall appear, we shall be like him; for we shall see him as he is (1 John 3:2)."

St. Paul also said, "For we know in part, and we prophesy in part. 10But when that which is perfect is come, then that which is in part shall be done away. 11When I was a child, I spake as a child, I understood as a child, I thought as a child: but when I became a man, I put away childish things. 12For now we see through a glass (into a mirror), darkly; but then face to face: now I know in part; but then shall I know even as also I am known (1 Corinthians 13:9-12)."

Considering the apostle's metaphor of looking into a dim mirror, I would like to pause for reflection and express how much I appreciate my son's insistence that this rambling study about "Death and Beyond" be written. Perhaps, some will read and recognize inspiration while others only see heresy. Regardless, I'm sure that more supporting Scriptures have been used in this short volume than any detractors might employ to bolster their "fuzzy ideology" about what occurs when life ends. A few critics might suggest that I have not "rightly divided the word of truth (2 Timothy 2:15)." Unfortunately, that verse is often used as a code for, "You did not read the text the same way I read the text to arrive at my exact opinion." However, based on the tedious number of biblical passages provided here, I have done my best in studying "to show myself approved unto God, a workman that needeth not to be ashamed (2 Timothy 2:15)." Possibly, if nothing else, I have sufficiently stirred the theological pot and motivated my skeptics to dig into God's Word for themselves and "make full proof of their ministry (2 Timothy 4:5)" as it applies to the afterlife.

God bless and protect you on your journey from here to there while always remembering to "give diligence to make your calling and election sure: for if ye do these things, ye shall never fall (2 Peter 1:10)." Or in modern terminology, "Do everything in your power to answer the call of God's election and have your name written in the Book of Life." Amen!

ABOUT THE AUTHOR

Edwin Woolsey has authored a total of twelve books. His "And There Were Giants" series is a fantasy adaptation of two horrendous apocalypses outlined in Genesis and the Revelation. The series' first two books, "Into the Land of Nede" and "Beyond the Gates of Daemon-gore," portray the rise of human culture and the universal destruction of Earth's earliest civilization. The last book, "Up from the Pit of Dudael," illustrates global events at the End of Time before Christ's Second Advent.

"If My People – God's Call for American Revival" compares the original founding of America to the history of ancient Israel and the commissioning of Christ's Church.

"The Voice Of Seven Thunders – Shadows of Things to Come" parallels the symbolism of the seven Jewish Holy Days in Leviticus, Chapter 23, with God's overall timeline for human history.

"The Revealing – Unlocking the Revelation of Jesus Christ" is a verse-by-verse analysis of the book of Revelation, comparing present world events to current doctrines of the Western Church.

The author's latest project is the Chronicler series, a novelized retelling of his family history from the time of the Saxon settlement of Roman Britannia to America's Great Depression. The first work in the six-book series is entitled,

"The Wolves of War." The second book is "Ivernia's Quest." The third book is called "Nova Anglia." The fourth book in the series is "Ashes, Ashes, We All Fall Down." The last book in the series is named, "Beyond the Father of Waters." The fifth book is yet to be announced.

Edwin Woolsey has three wonderful children, ages 33, 30, and 27. Now retired, Edwin was an educator in the Missouri Public School System for a total of 31 years. A lifelong student of the Bible, Mr. Woolsey serves as both teacher and pastor in his community. He is also a newspaper contributor. Some of the author's hobbies include gardening, fishing, hunting, and other nature activities. His interests in literature encompass history/archaeology and science fiction.

Visit the author at http://myauthorscorner.weebly.com/

Printed in the United States
by Baker & Taylor Publisher Services